#1 International Best Seller

Shattering Identity Bias

By Mona Shindy

Shattering Identity Bias

By Mona Shindy

By MONA SHINDY © Copyright
All rights reserved.
Book Layout ©2022
www.EvolveGlobalPublishing.com

No part of this book may be reproduced or transmitted in any form or by any means, electronic or mechanical, including photocopying, recording or by any information storage and retrieval system, without written permission from the author.

Limit of Liability Disclaimer: The information contained in this book is for information purposes only and may not apply to your situation. The author, publisher, distributor and provider provide no warranty about the content. The information provided is subjective. All links are for information purposes only and are not warranted for content, accuracy, or any other implied or explicit purpose.

Shattering Identity Bias by Mona Shindy
1st Edition. 2022
ASIN: B09SP2Q1FD (Amazon Kindle)
ISBN: 978-0-6452404-6-7 (eBook)
ISBN: 978-0-6454380-1-7 (Amazon Print)
ISBN: 978-0-6454380-0-0 (Ingram Spark) PAPERBACK
ISBN: 978-0-6454380-2-4 (Ingram Spark) HARDCOVER
ISBN: 978-0-6452404-6-7 (Smashwords)

CONTACT THE AUTHOR:
Author Website: www.monashindy.com
LinkedIn: https://www.linkedin.com/in/mona-shindy-84ba54121/

TRADEMARKS

All product names, logos, and brands are the property of their respective owners. All company, product and service names used in this book are for identification purposes only. The use of these names, logos, and brands does not imply endorsement. All other trademarks cited herein are the property of their respective owners.

Praise for 'Shattering Identity Bias'

In 'Shattering Identity Bias', Captain Mona Shindy, CSC, gets personal, professional and pensive. In relaying her family's early beginnings in Egypt to a life built post-migration in Australia, culminating in her decorated career in the Australian Navy, Shindy brings us on her journey. Her story is one peppered with tragedy, setbacks and grit, as well as resistance and conquest at each milestone. Racism, Islamophobia and misogyny permeate every facet of Australian society and Shindy, having been on the receiving end of all three as a visibly Arab and Muslim woman, does not hold back in sharing how her struggles made her stronger in her occupation of choice.

In addition to contending with external obstacles, Shindy shares how her intra-communal pressures as an officer during the Gulf War period caused her loyalty to be tested from both sides. Additionally, whilst raising a family in a career that demanded frequent time away from home, Shindy shares her experience of the perennial work-life balance struggle experienced by mothers, worldwide. Peeling back the often shiny façade of success to reveal the reality of tough choices is what makes this read so relatable.

It is clear from Shindy's story that her career and life trajectory have hinged upon principled decisions. Her commitment to integrity, her faith and her family, whilst excelling as the first Muslim woman Captain in the Australian Navy, are astonishing accomplishments. Amidst the cacophony of racism, Islamophobia, sexism and criticism, Shindy stood tall, exemplifying what it *means for institutions to be consciously inclusive. A role model for women, particularly women of colour, she has raised the bar of aspirational achievement.*

— **Tasneem Chopra OAM** (Diversity and Cross Cultural Consultant) —

A masterful memoir that delicately but honestly explores what it's like living at the nexus of reverence and rejection.

Mona's journey is more than a migrant's tale, it's also a cautionary one. It speaks to the conditions and criteria that determine who gets to be celebrated as an Australian.

Mona is a trailblazer who has spent decades fighting for her nation despite countless hurdles. And yet, she refuses to stop, irrespective of the personal cost, because Mona is determined to create pathways for others.

— **Antoinette Lattouf** (Author of How to Lose Friends and Influence White People, Speaker, Diversity Advocate and Journalist – TEN, ABC, SBS, Triple J and print press) —

Table of Contents

Praise for 'Shattering Identity Bias' 7
About The Author 11
Foreword 13
Author's Note 15
Prologue 19
Section 1 - The Path of Migrant Child to Navy Captain 25
   Chapter 1 - Emigration and Growing Up 27
      The Big Shift 27
      Settling In and Growing Up 33
      School Years 43
      'Unlucky' 53
      Grown Up Overnight 61
   Chapter 2 - The Early Career 69
      Leadership and Adventure 69
      Posted to Sea 85
      Fitting In 93
      Making My Mark 99
   Chapter 3 - Family, Marriage and Children 107
      Number 42 107
      Married Life 113

Chapter 4 - Organisational Leadership, War and Success 121
    Gaining Respect 121
    Being Away 129
    War 137
    Building and Supporting Navy Growth 149

Section 2 - Chief of Navy's Strategic Advisor on Islamic Cultural Affairs 159

Section 2: Introduction 161

Chapter 1 - An Awakening of Self (2013) 167

Chapter 2 - Cultural Reform - Not Everyone's Idea of a Good Thing (2013-2015) 181

Chapter 3 - Hijab (September 2014 onwards) 197

Chapter 4 - Media 209

Chapter 5 - Not my Navy – Reputation at All Costs 215

Chapter 6 - The Betrayal 227

Chapter 7 - Challenged Loyalties 235

Chapter 8 - Effecting Change - Political and Legal Involvement 241

Chapter 9 - Time's Up 251

Chapter 10 - Reflections 259

Final Words 269

References 273

About The Author

Captain Mona Shindy came from humble migrant beginnings. Having emigrated from Egypt with her family at the age of three, she watched her parents work selflessly, giving everything they had to ensure their children grew up strong, successful and happy.

Drawing on her parents' teachings, Mona's life has been characterised by hard work, education and a strong belief and desire to openly live all aspects of her identity and be accepted in traditionally separated environments. In doing so, she has taken many paths not well-trodden and forged roads never before traversed to become a highly successful strategic leader, engineer, project director, change agent and author, confidently shattering many stereotypes about who society believed she should be. In 2015, Mona was awarded a Conspicuous Service Cross in the Australia Day Honours List for outstanding service as a strategic intercultural advisor and later that year was announced as National Telstra Business Woman of the Year.

Mona's story is one of courage, being true to oneself and carving out a path to success against the odds. In the process, she has created a legacy that is both inspiring to minorities and educative for organisations serious about addressing blind spots to get the best out of all employees and target markets.

Drawing on over thirty years of experience as a Naval Officer, strategic leader, business director, change agent and engineering executive, and utilising strong academic credentials and the lessons and skills gained throughout a truly inspiring career; Captain Mona Shindy now imparts knowledge to others as a highly sought-after author, international keynote speaker, mentor and strategic leadership and management consultant.

Foreword

Mona's is an important Australian story. It is the story of the first female Muslim to serve in the Royal Australian Navy. It is one from which much can be learned and that demonstrates the strong desire of migrants to contribute and the challenges they face. It is a story of crossing boundaries: moving country, traversing communities and navigating cultures.

Shattering Identity Bias details the incredible personal work required to move between seemingly disparate groups and navigate the challenges of being seen (and asked) to represent these groups, while at the same time not feeling that any one of these groups truly reflects who she is.

What is striking in Mona's story are her experiences of belonging; the reader is taken on Mona's journey of finding her 'self' and her sense of place. It is at once joyful – the camaraderie of her early years in the Navy, the accolades bestowed upon her as she became the face of diversity in the ADF – and painful when we learn of the very tenuous nature of being different, where trust and belonging can be lost in an instant.

So much of Mona's story has been invisible until now.

In being given roles that furthered her visibility as a migrant, a woman, a Muslim and a Naval Officer, Mona had a very public presence. She was encouraged to speak up and speak out and enabled to do so in representative roles in the ADF. But being encouraged and enabled do not necessarily equate to being empowered. As Mona's story reveals, she was able to take risks, but they were risks for her alone. If she faltered, the safety net of belonging was not always there. Deeply entrenched power dynamics in an organisation such as Defence are near impossible for one person to move alone.

As Mona questions the powerful influencers in her life – cultural, religious, institutional and familial – she reveals what is both gained and lost in the process. Importantly, her story raises questions for those doing 'diversity and inclusion' work – and poses an uncomfortable question: who really is benefiting? If organisational goals do not focus on those whose 'diversity' they set out to target and achieve, then what is the point?

There is no doubt that the many communities of which Mona has been a part have benefited greatly from her involvement and her work will continue to be a beacon for those who follow in her footsteps.

Dr Samantha Crompvoets

Author's Note

❖

When I think back to my childhood, I know with absolute certainty that my parents' unconditional belief in me was instrumental in laying the strong foundations that have since supported and guided many of my life decisions and actions. I took on challenges that might have been easier to avoid. I enjoyed learning about the world and dreaming up solutions to problems I observed. I loved the logic of mathematics and the sciences and competed relentlessly in all sporting fields. I chose to speak when many others were silent.

I have written this book as a way of giving back. A thank you to those who raised and inspired me and as a resource for those who follow after me. My life's journey has not been easy by any stretch of the imagination, nor has it been straightforward. It regularly involved scenarios where I either found or voluntarily placed myself among the 'minority' in a much larger and generally more uniform community of people. I have always followed my passions, and in doing so, have developed a unique identity shaped by many different inputs from the various communities to which I belong. However, with their long-established cultural beliefs and biases, some members of these different communities have been quite challenged by my presence among them.

With its many different sects, negative experiences with foreign militaries in ancestral lands and various interpretations of what are appropriate roles for both men and women, the Muslim community sometimes grapples with biases directed at members who seek to deviate from long-held cultural norms and understanding. It has adherents who struggle with the notion of Muslims serving in the Australian Defence Force and women working, particularly in any male-dominated arenas, let alone in the profession of arms.

Likewise, the Australian Defence Force is still a relatively homogenous community, unfamiliar with Muslims in its structure. The ADF continues to learn and benefit from the different ideas and understanding this portion of Australian society can provide. It has ongoing work to do so that one day its constituents at all ranks can be more representative of the entire Australian demographic it serves.

Although powerfully beneficial and advantageous for the growth of any group, diversity of thought and perspective is not always easily understood or accepted by the majority. It requires an investment of extra energy to accommodate and learn from differences; something not everyone easily affords. Consequently, I have encountered many people and events that have challenged my cherished values and sense of justice throughout my life. Prejudice and dismissiveness can ignite negative feelings of regret or bitterness in the most resilient of us and lead to less than optimal outcomes for all. Having rationalised and overcome many such scenarios, I am now more passionate and committed than ever to sharing the lessons I have learned along the way in order to benefit others.

It is my strong hope that the significant emotional toll I endured while navigating my various communities and responding to obstacles presented to my advocated changes in attitudes and practice will help support others to forge their own unique paths and identities and achieve what might traditionally have been considered an unrealistic potential. My journey, deviating from well-established institutional norms over the years, has come at a significant personal cost to me. I have been hurt by hostility and rejection. I have been ridiculed, devalued and, on occasions, ignored or not even seen. I have struggled for space and acceptance in communities I love, but that have not always loved me back.

Shattering Identity Bias

In writing *Shattering Identity Bias*, I have sought to provide insight into why and how external interventions must be utilised to help identify and then dismantle structural norms that permit powerful networks to act with impunity. I want to demonstrate that without robust, documented, data-informed, transparent and externally and independently contestable and defensible policy and practices, conservative 'total institutions', such as Defence, will find it near impossible to effect meaningful and necessary reforms. Cultural norms permeate from the top, and where power imbalances are entrenched by design, and reputation is guarded at all costs, strong disincentives for change exist. Similarly, where Muslim women and their allies do not challenge long-held cultural norms in some homes and societies not supported by religious law, then disadvantages and stifling will persist.

This is my story of courage in the face of, at times, extreme bias. A bias that stemmed from all the different communities I sought to belong to. It is my story of taking paths less trodden and forging new roads never before traversed; my story of integrity, resilience and grit. It is a story in which I realise great success and influence change while remaining true to myself. At times, it is tainted with sadness, frustration and prejudice. It is full of lessons told with complete honesty and vulnerability. While I have sought to document difficulties I encountered in the various communities I belong to, I must also acknowledge the genuine support and strong investment many members of those communities made in me. No group is perfect. Individually, we only know what we have been exposed to and by working together, and sharing ideas and experiences, everyone benefits and grows. There are no regrets but there is an immense amount of pride.

Shattering Identity Bias is a story for women and for minorities whom I hope will relate to and learn from the many scenarios covered. It is also a story for organisations and academics who wish to understand the challenges faced by minority groups in order to optimise outcomes in work environments and, more broadly, in society.

Ultimately, however, *Shattering Identity Bias* is a story of hope for the future.

Mona Shindy

Prologue

When I reflect on how my parents migrated from Egypt to Australia in the early 70s, I marvel at their courage and adventurous spirit. My father, Ezz-El-Din, and mother, Aida, were young professionals with secure government jobs in Cairo. Dad was a prosecutor and Mum a social worker. They met at a bus stop every morning on their commute to work. My father was very social, so I imagine him striking up a conversation with an attractive and stylish young lady as they waited for the bus. In those days, Egyptian women were very influenced by English and French fashion. My mother, an absolute stunner both inside and out, most certainly would have been turning heads with her salon-straightened hair, pressed business suit and matching belt, purse and shoes.

It wasn't long before they were married and the parents of three energetic youngsters. I was the sassy and confident girl between my two brothers, Hassan and Mohamed. I did everything my brothers did, though I suspect I got away with a little more.

I felt very loved and inspired by my parents. Mum enjoyed dressing me up in the best clothes the family could afford and Dad never stopped boosting my confidence with everything he said. I was his little princess who would one day change the world.

"Monameeno, al-ageeba, al-azeema."

Dad said this to me almost every day. Monameeno was a play on the name *Farafeero* – a cartoon superhero mouse who regularly starred in the Egyptian equivalent to Australia's *Play School*. Farafeero was a cute little unassuming character who would always miraculously survive in arduous circumstances and triumph against the most scrupulous of villains. He was a problem-solver and a kind-hearted social advocate, committed to assisting others and making a positive difference in the world. I loved that little rodent! Very attuned to the way this cartoon character made me think, feel and imagine, my father always encouraged me to believe I could do the same. Hence, I became Monameeno. The rest of the phrase, '*al-ageeba, al-azeema*', translates from Arabic to mean 'the lovable, the great one'.

To Dad, I was Mona, the lovable and the great.

My parents had great hopes and dreams for my brothers and me. We were all going to university. It was an expectation and they would do everything in their power to ensure our comfort and success. Mum and Dad taught me about love and sacrifice. From as early as I can recall, it was always about us and our needs.

I was born in a downtown apartment with the help of my uncle who was a young doctor. My mother tells me that the whole building and most of the street knew I was entering the world as she screamed with each contraction. Responsible for registering my birth, my father officially recorded a day at the beginning of October, rather than late September when I was actually born. He used to be paid at the beginning of each month and was adamant he needed to have sufficient funds to buy me nice gifts each year. Even as highly educated professionals in secure government work, their pay cheques only covered essential expenses and they had no real prospects for getting ahead. This was one of the social challenges that drove their decision to emigrate.

At this time, my father and mother were in their early thirties. My older brother had just turned three, I was two and my younger brother was only a few months old. My parents had been working for almost a decade and had no savings to speak of. They could not see how they could position themselves to give us, their children, the opportunities they never had.

My father started completing emigration applications at a number of Western embassies. The whole process of assessment, interviews and medical evaluations took approximately a year. We also had to obtain letters of support and sponsorship from my mother's older sister, who had emigrated to the USA, and one of my father's distant cousins, who'd emigrated to Australia.

As it turned out, my family were accepted to both the USA and Australia.

Having excelled at English through school, my father was eager to sow new roots in a foreign land and his research swayed him towards Australia. The migration journey was a closely held secret between my parents and their sponsors abroad. They knew their families wouldn't let them go if they found out about their plans. My father went ahead on an exploratory mission. Some months later, a letter arrived in the mail telling of 'the most beautiful place on Earth'. He had arrived in the abundant and enchanting land of Australia's Gadigal people, also now known as Sydney, Australia. In the correspondence, Dad asked Mum to sell everything, resign from her job and bring the kids.

Dad had found work as a cleaning hand at a chemical processing factory in Mascot. He'd rented a small rundown two-bedroom unit in the adjoining suburb of Botany, walking distance from the factory and a few short kilometres from the airport. It wasn't much, he said, but it was more than enough to house the warm atmosphere of love between siblings and parents.

So began a new chapter – for me and for all of us. It was a chapter that was to bring much growth, new opportunities and knowledge about how the world looked and functioned outside the borders of Egypt. This chapter saw my parents sacrifice their careers, their respected positions in society and the comfort of warm family bonds and interactions so their children could achieve everything they dreamed about. With the sacrifices came new experiences of unexpected friendships, hard-earned successes and joy, as well as prejudice, fear and alienation.

With a positive and hopeful outlook on life, I achieved many things for which I am immensely proud. My journey, however, was never as easy as Farafeero's seemed to be. Coupled with the joyful successes, there were many setbacks and events that evoked great sadness and frustration.

I saw my parents struggle with many things I had not noticed before. They both seemed to work very hard. I'm sure Dad had two jobs and Mum spent a lifetime recounting her dreadful experiences working the nightshift for a year in a wool factory. Eventually, she got another job in a rubber factory doing the afternoon shift. I remember this time clearly because she would occasionally bring home those small colourful balls that would go missing after the first bounce.

We had no extended family close by and my parents would share childcare duties in such a way that they were hardly ever together, except on weekends. They would both tell stories of how people at work bossed them around or spoke to them like children because they had accents and sometimes misunderstood unfamiliar phrases. They didn't seem as happy as they were before. They were, without a doubt, exhausted and rundown.

Sometimes, I overheard conversations in which they both expressed regrets about migrating and yearned for an opportunity to return to Egypt. I suspect they were initially trapped with insufficient funds to even pay for return flights. Mum was really worried about us losing the ability to communicate in Arabic. She had brought lots of children's books with her and, in the early days, spent many hours teaching us the Arabic alphabet and how to read. She invested a lot of time in educating us on many aspects of Egyptian history and culture. I'm sure we were more informed and more proud of our heritage than most teenagers in Egypt!

Besides dealing with their own struggles in the new environment, my parents were perhaps most challenged by situations where we, as children, encountered negative comments or attitudes. They worked hard to shield us from the views of some who saw our family as a threat to their opportunities or way of life. When they couldn't, these scenarios would be met with assertive protests from my father, who could become quite incensed at the blatant and prevalent intolerance that accompanied our early days as 'wogs'. Then there was the extended family back in Egypt, some of whom were convinced my parents would lose their values and their children's future in an unknown foreign land, far away from a strong and visible Islamic culture. They copped it from all directions. It was their first real experience straddling communities – trying to belong to both and trying to work out how to make pluralism work.

For us kids, it was all about the neighbourhood children, many of whom also came from varied corners of the world. In the main, we all loved playing together. It was only when disagreements arose that the influence and ideas of their parental communities would become apparent, like an excretion of venom. At times, they could be very cruel and unaccepting of differences. Many biases and conflicts stemming from other locations and times around the world had somehow been etched into the minds of our new playmates. Some had issues with our skin colour and religion, while others were repulsed by what we chose to eat.

"You are black and ugly. My dad says you are dirty," one child proclaimed.

"Muslims are going to hell! You lot killed so many Christians by starting the crusades," another declared with a more than slightly skewed recount of historical events.

"You are a gollywog," was another line I heard almost daily in the early days. And then, of course, the most common phrase used to exclude and *other* was generally delivered by the kids with an Anglo-Celtic heritage who would, when angry, tell us, "Go back to where you came from!"

They spoke with such certainty and conviction that Australia was a white man's land. It didn't seem to matter that we might have been Australian citizens for longer than them or that the Aboriginal owners had inhabited the continent for tens of thousands of years before any of us were even born.

Through the many tears and fights, my parents were always available and ready to console and educate. They were steadfast in their dedication to a vision of creating the very best outcomes for their children. They made so many sacrifices, showered us with endless love and were nothing less than a wonderful inspiration.

Section 1
The Path of Migrant Child to Navy Captain

Mona Shindy

Chapter 1
Emigration and Growing Up

The Big Shift

I remember landing at Sydney Airport and standing by the carousels, waiting for the luggage. At seven o'clock in the morning, the airport was awash with moving bodies, all in a rush to their next destination and wanting to be first to get their bags off the carousel. It was like the central train station in Cairo but without the many different merchants jostling for attention and unceremoniously shoving handfuls of merchandise in everyone's face. The people here looked different to those back in Egypt. I couldn't understand much of what was being said around me and only picked up the odd word or two from people who had just stepped off the same plane as us. I felt very small and fragile between the legs of those crowded around me. Most appeared focused on things other than their present surroundings and I sensed a real danger in potentially being crushed.

It was not long before I heard the carousel belt we were loitering around begin to move. We jumped up and looked at the hole in the wall, waiting. Mum had explained that the big bags, with all our clothes, would soon appear and we would need to pull them off the belt. We were ready. As suitcase after suitcase began to emerge, I wrinkled my nose at the mix of new rubber from the belt and the strong and impatient odour of perspiration.

It wasn't just our clothes in those suitcases; they contained everything we owned. Before we left, Mum had also purchased a green leather coat and a gold locket that held a tiny copy of the Holy Quran. Essentially, these were the only possessions my parents' savings could buy.

Carrying Mohamed in her arms, Mum shielded her one-year-old from the busy world we now found ourselves in. Hassan and I hung onto her green coat so tightly that our knuckles were white with tension. Mohamed looked a lot more comfortable and safe than Hassan and I felt, with so many strange bodies scraping by us and pushing us around. At one point, I thought Hassan was going to cry and the very sight of his face made me start to panic. I drew him even closer to me and patted his back in an attempt to reassure him and myself that everything would be okay.

Mum had a way of catastrophising the potential consequences in any given situation. "You'll be lost forever with no one to look after you," she'd said, warning us many times of the perils of becoming separated from her. Lost and on our own, starving and dying a slow death on the streets of a strange land. That would be the scenario unless, of course, we were murdered more quickly. We understood.

I couldn't help myself staring at the people around me. Many were very fair, with colourful eyes and light hair. It was so weird. Occasionally, someone caught my eye and I'd look away. Some threw kind smiles our way. Others, probably as intrigued by our appearance as I was by theirs, observed us from a distance. I suspect we looked pretty cute with our chubby cheeks, olive skin and curly black hair.

Hassan and I each carried our own piece of hand luggage that contained a few activities to keep us busy on the long flight and our personal baby toilet trainers. Yes, those little plastic bowls! Thinking back, I wonder if maybe the social worker in Mum reasoned that keeping things as familiar as possible would somehow make the trip easier. I don't think they did and it was really difficult carrying those large handbags. Apart from that, I don't think we used anything from the bags. The colouring books and pencils the stewards gave us on the plane were much more interesting and, as it turned out, the big toilets in the airports and on the plane were more practical, even though we had to grab hold around Mum's knees so we didn't fall in. An adult and three children crammed together into one tiny cubicle certainly made for some 'interesting' scenarios – not to mention smelly ones.

The overwhelm of our first plane trip and the excitement of seeing Dad again, meant we ate nothing all the way to Singapore. We just couldn't. It wasn't until we were on the flight from Singapore to Sydney that we finally ate, polishing off everything the stewards put in front of us. Mum's delight and relief, however, quickly turned into shock upon the discovery we'd eaten pork!

As we waited at the carousels, mesmerised as suitcase after suitcase glided by, I noticed Mum talking to another passenger. They were speaking in English so, try as I might, I couldn't understand a single thing they were saying, but I didn't need to. With the perceptiveness of a toddler, I knew Mum was uncomfortable. Not only uncomfortable but scared. All three of us fell silent, standing as still as stone until Mum pulled us away.

As it turned out, this person had been a kind-hearted local gentleman, not the weird, deviant murderer we'd assumed he was.

Many years later, Mum told us what he'd said. "Can I give you a lift somewhere, love?"

It had been the word 'love' that had Mum reeling. She was wearing a wedding ring and had three toddlers hanging on to her as she struggled with large suitcases. He'd merely been offering help, not propositioning Mum in the most brazen of ways as she'd thought.

Mum had been petrified. This was just the first of many conversations she would engage in where she'd assume the worst only to be pleasantly surprised later.

New experiences, challenges, mistakes, misunderstandings and growth – so began our new life.

Finally, dragging suitcases and hand luggage, we exited to the waiting area. It had been months since I'd seen my father. An eternity to a toddler. My eyes raced from side to side, scanning the crowd. I couldn't see him at all. Had he forgotten when we were arriving? Had I forgotten what he looked like?

"Aida!" A voice called my mother's name. Excited and happy. "Aida!"

There he was. Right at the front of the waiting crowd. He looked different. The three-piece suit I remembered him always wearing had been replaced by dark sunglasses, jeans and a T-shirt.

In the months Dad had been gone, Mum had filled our time with hundreds of stories of good moments together and the promise of new adventures when we were reunited. We weren't going to wait any longer. Hassan started running and within seconds had latched onto Dad's legs. I wasn't far behind.

"Baba!" I launched myself at him, screaming with delight.

"Monameeno!" Dad swept me up into his arms and suddenly everything about him was familiar.

I grabbed one of Dad's earlobes as I'd done so often back in Egypt. They were big, warm and soft, and somehow, brought me instant comfort and happiness. He looked at me and I knew, without a doubt, that Dad had also missed our small but very personal moments.

I was somewhere completely foreign to everything I had known but, at that moment, I was instantly home.

Mona Shindy

Settling In and Growing Up

Our first home was a basic unit on the main road through Botany. Five of us, squashed into two bedrooms, a single bathroom, a living area and a tiny kitchen. The windows were small but did not keep out the noise of the traffic from the main road – cars, buses and trucks heading in and out of the factories all day and all night.

It was a four-storey building, red brick, with no lifts. Of course, our unit was on the top level so trudging up those stairs every day, our little legs would really be struggling by the end. Mohamed and I would go grocery shopping with Mum while Hassan was at school. It was a challenge carrying the bags of food up four flights, but we wanted to help. It was worth it because then Mum would cook. We were always part of the activities that went on at home. We particularly loved watching her cook and loved learning how to prepare meals. The Middle Eastern aromas and smell of the spices just took us right back to Egypt.

I shared a bedroom with my brothers. Three of us in one tiny room with just enough space for a bunk bed for Hassan and Mohamed on one side and a single bed up against the opposite wall for me. There were no built-in wardrobes so once we got the tallboy and the dresser in, there was virtually no room to move other than to walk in there and hop into bed. That was it.

Our bedtime routine was something I loved. We'd eat together as a family, then it was bath time and under the covers by 6:30 pm. Every night.

"Hurry up kids," Dad ordered, as though there was some urgency about us being in bed exactly on time.

"Good night," Mum said as she turned the light off and shut the door. We knew our parents expected us to stay in bed and we did but, of course, once that door shut, we'd start talking. We were close as siblings and could talk about everything and anything – sharing stories of our day.

Hassan would start by talking about his school day – the new friends he'd made, people he saw and the things he learned. Food the other kids had in their lunchboxes was often a topic.

"Sandwiches," he'd say. "They all have sandwiches." And he'd describe the ones he'd seen kids eating that day. Vegemite and butter on white bread. Hundreds and thousands. Peanut butter sandwiches cut into squares or triangles.

"Why don't they eat what we eat?" I'd say.

We talked about our struggles, too. Our worries about things we didn't understand and tricky words with strange meanings. Sometimes Hassan talked about the other kids teasing him about his smelly lunchbox.

Usually, while we were talking, we'd also hear Dad giggling as he watched The Benny Hill Show on our tiny black and white television. That TV was where we all received a lot of our early English education, watching cartoons and Australian shows like Play School.

When Hassan had finished talking about his day, Mohamed and I would tell him about the adventures we'd had with Mum. We'd describe our cooking and what we saw when we were out shopping.

"Mohamed got lost today," I remember telling Hassan one night. Like lots of little kids, I think he'd been caught up looking at the toys in the shop windows. "One minute he was there and the next Mum was going crazy because he was gone."

She'd started screaming and running down the street with me in tow, asking everyone we saw if they'd seen him.

"We couldn't find you for ages," I said to Mohamed. "Then we saw you with that man and he was holding your hand and walking the other way."

The man stopped when Mum screamed at him. "You're very lucky, lady," he'd said. "Very lucky."

"That's why we always have to stay with Mum," I said. "Because Mohamed nearly got stolen and we don't want to be stolen."

We were all very serious and quiet then. Like it always did, silence and no responses meant the day was over and our only option was to sleep.

Mum and Dad both worked very hard and played tag team looking after the family and venturing out for work. They were on a wealth-building mission. That year was challenging for them both. With no extended family support in Australia and not being comfortable leaving us in a care situation, they persevered with this arrangement until I joined my older brother at school.

We'd been in the Botany unit for about a year and a half when Mum and Dad announced we were moving. They'd secured the purchase of an old, three-bedroom weatherboard house in Mascot. I'd done a year in Kindergarten by this stage so, for Hassan and me, the move to Mascot also meant moving schools and having to make a ten-minute walk through several streets rather than just popping over to the adjacent building.

We loved this walk, though. Not only was it part of our routine but each day we'd stop at the local newsagent to get a Caramello Koala to top off the massive breakfast Mum had already made for us – eggs and toast, or foul muddamas (a fava bean porridge), or ta'ameya (Egyptian falafels). Whatever she prepared for us, you could be sure it was solid and filling, but we could always squeeze in a Caramello Koala.

The backyard of our new house seemed to go on forever. It was long and narrow and had two sheds. We kept chickens in one and the other was where Dad kept some tools, like the lawnmower and our bike.

That little red bike was like our ticket to fame because it was the only one in our neighbourhood. We saw that opportunity and would sell rides on the bike.

"Two cents," we'd say. "You can go up and down the street a couple of times." Kids would be lining up in the street, with their two cents in hand, ready for their turn.

That was just the beginning of our entrepreneurship.

It was hot waiting for a bike ride so we got the idea to start selling lemonade too. We'd sell it on street corners around the neighbourhood. Sometimes, we'd pick some flowers, walk to the shops and sell them to the local hairdresser for twenty cents.

We found lots of ways to collect a few cents here and there. Eventually, we would save enough to walk down to the local corner store and buy paper bags filled with lollies. There were all kinds of lollies in these bags – from gummy teeth to raspberry drops. My favourites were the liquorice bullets – the hard liquorice sticks coated in chocolate. They're still my favourites.

We were outside all the time, particularly in summer. We'd make our own pool – all we needed was Dad's old tarp and a heap of bricks, which we'd use to make the shape of an elevated rectangle. Then, we'd put the tarpaulin in the middle, fill it up with water and invite all the neighbourhood kids over. We knew we were as cool as could be because we had a tarp swimming pool in this big backyard and everyone could come over for a swim.

Cubby houses were another favourite and we were always building them. We used to get the job of cutting the grass. With such a huge yard, this would take us all day but it was worth it because of the major reward dad would give us at the end – a two-litre bottle of Coca-Cola! After going through the whole process of cutting the grass and raking it all up, we'd just sit down and enjoy our reward in our cubby house.

Our backyard also had an outdoor toilet. "It's called 'the dunny'," our Aussie neighbours told us. We'd never heard anything like that before, but we did what they said and called it 'the dunny'. We learned a lot of Australian slang from our neighbours; they were instrumental in helping us learn English and teaching us about the colonial influence in the shaping of Australian identity at the time.

Mascot was actually a very culturally diverse community. We had Anglo Saxon neighbours and further down the street we had Italian and Greek friends, whose parents were even more out of their depth than ours were. We were part of a huge melting pot of differing attitudes, beliefs, foods and traditions.

From time to time, we fought with other kids in the neighbourhood who would unwittingly offend us with their different perspectives and opinions. There was also taunting, as kids do, about the food we ate and the clothes we wore.

Mum used to dress us in each other's clothes sometimes. "Wasn't your brother wearing those pants last week? Why are you wearing them?" It wasn't uncommon for me to hear such comments and, as we got older, we became more aware of them. We were tough though and generally carried on pretending to be completely unperturbed until someone went just a little too far. In many ways, we ruled the streets around our block. I was an unapologetic tomboy and remember being in several fistfights growing up.

Our relationships within the neighbourhood were, however, predominantly positive. We played cricket and soccer with the local kids in the park and sold rides on our little red bike. Everyone got along.

Mrs Burbridge was one of our neighbours and she was lovely. I think she felt sorry for us because we didn't celebrate Christmas as Muslims. No tree or lights on the house like other families in the street, and no presents. She would go out and buy presents for us.

She was also the neighbour who coined Mohamed's Aussie name – Peter. Our family nickname for him was 'Bida' so when people asked Mohamed what his name was, he'd always say, "I'm Bida." It was a strange name to Australian ears and the closest thing they could come to was 'Peter'. Mrs Burbridge started it and it spread through the neighbourhood. We'd just giggle every time someone called him Peter, which probably didn't help.

The other thing we had, thanks to Mum and Dad's feverish work life, was a car. Not everyone had a car on our street but somehow we did and it was something else that made us cool with the other kids.

EMB 180 – that was the number plate on it. A rusty green Holden station wagon, but being a good old Aussie car, it did us well. Dad was proud of that car and we spent many weekends helping him scrape back the rust and fill the gaps with putty. He'd sandpaper it back and spray-paint it. He never managed to get a colour that matched exactly. I'm not sure he even tried or asked the manufacturer. He just went along to Bunnings and bought whatever he thought looked the closest. Over time, the car became a complete hodgepodge of colours.

One year, he even got the house paint out. We'd spent ages scraping back all the rust, a huge job, and spray paint is expensive. "We'll just use this," he said and started slapping it on. There were darker patches of green and lighter patches but he just kept going until the car looked more like a camouflaged army vehicle.

Patchy paint and rust aside, that car brought us new-found freedom to venture out on weekends. Our favourite place in summer was Maroubra Beach. We'd have to get going early so we could get one of those shacks that lined the grassy area in front of the beach. Mum would lay out our food on the table inside the shack and we'd spend the day playing in the sand, swimming and sitting on the timber chairs in the shack eating the feast Mum always prepared.

Each shack had four quadrants, so there was enough space for four families. We met a lot of people that way. Sometimes, we'd offer people a taste of our food and they'd offer theirs. There was always a fair bit of interest in what we were eating, as well as some hesitation because we had food people just hadn't seen before. The seagulls didn't care though. They'd come squawking and hovering around, hustling for scraps. Sometimes they were quite bold and just strutted up and stole stuff right off the table.

Mona Shindy

The shacks always smelled of fish and chips. Then we'd come along with our Middle Eastern spices and the two would mingle. It was an interesting combination.

We weren't strong swimmers. Cairo isn't coastal so learning to swim there wasn't really a priority. Usually, we just paddled around, playing in the waves and staying close to the shoreline. Floating was the extent of my swimming expertise, which was a good thing actually because, on one terrifying day, I got caught in a rip.

I was convinced I was going to die. One minute, I was playing in the shallows, the next, I couldn't touch the bottom. I struggled against it for a while but then gave up. It's all over, I thought. I'm never getting back to Mum and Dad and my brothers. Giving up may have saved me because I relaxed. I floated. Then a wave washed over my face and I could touch the bottom.

At the time, I had no idea how lucky I was. I do now. Swimming is still not one of my stronger skills. Later, in the navy, I was made to do six months of swimming lessons as part of my training. It helped. I passed the swim test but I'd always say to the captain on any ship I joined, "If I'm the person overboard and you don't see me actually fall, just keep going because I'm unlikely to survive for longer than a few minutes."

They were fun times, those weekends at the beach. Fun, despite my experience with the rip. Despite the sharp rocks that cut my thigh open. Despite the bluebottles and the time Hassan swam right into a whole school of them and had to be taken up to the surf club and doused with vinegar and warm water. It was all part of Australian life. Stressful for Mum, but for us kids, it was all part of the adventure.

Mum was always anxious about Dad driving and the dangers of travelling too far. The thing is – Dad didn't actually have a licence at first and had never learned to drive. It's a testament to how things were back then – a lot more laid back. We were all in the car when he picked it up after buying it and we drove off, really excited. The next thing we knew, we were off the road and heading for the local pub. Dad drove straight into it.

Luckily, there wasn't too much damage to the pub but the car's bumper bar was another matter. Of course, Dad wanted to fix it himself. There were quite a few 'discussions' between Mum and Dad around that time, but it didn't stop us from getting out and about; we even made it up to Brisbane and the Gold Coast.

With Dad doing all the maintenance on the car, I don't know how we kept it on the road for so long or how it passed inspection. But it did and it served us well.

Our early years were hard but happy and we were blessed to be immersed in what was becoming a growing multicultural society. A lot of what we went through then – how we coped and adjusted, what we were taught by our parents – has shaped who I became as an adult. There's no regret there, only strength and the love of family.

Mona Shindy

School Years

The harsh clang of the brass bell signalled the end of school lunchtime play. I searched for Hassan in the crowd traipsing back inside but the playground was a sea of similar uniforms. Two bigger students had hold of the bell, gripping its long, wooden handle as they swung it up and down until the last straggler passed them by.

"I want to ring that bell," said Mohamed as we peered through our window at the scene below.

"One day, it will be our turn," I answered. I wanted to ring that bell too.

This was our daily ritual. At four years of age, I was fascinated by what went on at my brother's school that adjoined our home.

The school drop-off was busy and bustling. People walked in and out of the building. Blue buses pulled up and offloaded streams of uniformed kids in a sea of grey – shirts, shorts and tunics. Younger children walked in the gate, hand-in-hand with their mothers, slipped out of the cars that lined the road out the front of the school or glided by on bicycles.

The playground filled slowly as the minutes ticked by. Clusters of children played while parents stood in groups having a chat. Many of the girls skipped with long ropes; boys hung about or chased each other, playing rough and tumble games.

At recess and lunch, again we raced to watch as kids poured out of the two-storey brick building or one of the several outbuildings dotted around the grounds. Again, they'd mill around – congregating under trees, playing tips, skipping, playing handball and soccer. There was a lot to do. A teacher would wander slowly around, followed by the bell-ringers who lugged that huge bell, waiting for their cue to start it clanging.

I was torn between being desperate to start school and not wanting to change my life as it was now. I loved my daily routine – walking Hassan to school, going shopping, cooking with Mum, Arabic lessons. At the same time, I longed to be part of the hustle and bustle; to have access to the library and all those books, and to join in with the games and activities Hassan sometimes described in our night-time chats.

Then there were the other stories Hassan occasionally shared. His sadness and frustration at not being able to understand so many things; at being at the bottom of his class; at his reports that detailed everything he had to do to improve.

Our huge Arabic–English dictionary got an absolute flogging. Hassan was always poring over it. "How do I say this word?" he'd ask, pointing to the word 'schedule'. "Is it sh-edule or sk-edule?" He wanted to get it right. He wanted to speak 'correctly'. He had this fear of not understanding and not being understood. There was a lot of apprehension on his part and I knew he was struggling. I was a little bit afraid myself; worried I would be exactly the same as him. So, I wanted to start school and, at the same time, I didn't.

The day did finally come, though.

Proudly, I walked the short distance to school with my mum and Hassan. A brand new tunic and my springy black hair in two neat plaits. Instead of green or blue ribbon to match the tunic, like the other girls had, my plaits were woven through with strands of yellow or brown cotton or wool – whatever Mum was knitting with at the time – and then tied up in neat bunches. It was cute but different.

That first week went by in a whirl of excitement and confusion. I understood only a little of what was being said around me but tried the best I could to join in. Our classroom had a big blackboard at the front and pinboards on the wall where our work would get put up with thumbtacks in each corner. Little wooden chairs and desks, with lids that lifted up so we could put our pencils, textas and bits of paper inside, were organised in neat rows and we had a large space at the front that was used for floor-time.

Floor-time was one of my favourite activities because we'd all sit cross-legged in front of the teacher while she read us a story. Sometimes, there would be a thumbtack stuck in the mat; one the teacher had dropped or someone had swiped from the pinboard.

Sitting and listening to a story one day in the first week, I felt a sharp prick at the top of my leg. "Ow," I cried out. Nobody heard me. I spent the rest of the afternoon trying to listen to the story and be brave at the same time. But I went home, crying.

"Somebody put a pin in me," I told Mum.

The next day, Mum came all the way to school with me and into the classroom. I'm pretty sure she told the teacher someone had been hurting me although nothing more was said.

Mum was constantly worried about us when we were at school. Were we warm enough? Did we have enough to eat? As a girl, it was also important to Mum that I be dressed appropriately, which meant wearing shorts under my tunic so nobody could see my undies should my skirt ride up a little.

Appropriate clothing also meant being warm enough. Not only did this mean having to wear a T-shirt under my tunic, which made me a bit of a nerd, but it also occasionally led to an impromptu midday visit from Mum.

One such day, when I was in Kindy, the sunny, mild morning had made way to a bitter wind sometime between recess and lunch. We were all busy with our work, wondering whether it would rain or if we would get outside to play at lunchtime, when there was a knock at the classroom door.

"I'm sorry to interrupt," a familiar voice said.

No! I didn't want to look. Nobody's mum ever came into the school. Not in the middle of the day.

"Excuse me but I just want to put this jumper on my daughter because I think she is probably cold."

Stunned, I sat there at my desk while my mother walked over. "Stand up, Mona," she said and, amidst giggles and wide-eyed stares, she helped me put a jumper on over my uniform, thanked my teacher and left.

Even though I knew, deep down, it came from a place of love, it was just another thing that made us different.

School was challenging in the early days. At first, my English skills were limited. I could say 'hello' to greet people and I knew a few essential verbs like 'play', 'run', 'eat' and 'come'. Mixing with the kids in our neighbourhood and watching TV had taught me a smattering of Aussie slang and a few choice swear words – that was it though. I knew some basic Arabic because Mum and Dad had been teaching me at home but as for the English alphabet or numbers, I was completely clueless.

We did get ESL classes at school. In our early years, we'd be taken by another teacher to get some extra help with English to try and assist us to catch up with the other kids.

Mum and Dad also tried to help at home. They spoke to us in Arabic and in English and tried to make our learning as enjoyable as possible.

"*Hosaan,*" Dad would suddenly say. "Quick! What is it in English?"

We'd all have to scrabble in our minds for an answer.

"Cow," Hassan shouted.

"No, no – it's horse," I said.

"Mona's got it," Dad said. "Okay, next one …"

On we went, a race to be the first with the correct answer. Later, we practised our maths the same way. Brothers against sister in a friendly, yet serious, competition.

Whenever Mum or Dad had a spare half hour, we'd sit down and do some reading or other practice with flashcards. We were learning Arabic and English simultaneously and it was a bit confusing at times but every bit helped and it kept us motivated and positive.

Mona Shindy

We did a lot of singing at school, which was lovely except the words were hard to wrap my mouth around. There were so many of them I didn't understand. Every morning, we would all sing Advance Australia Fair. That anthem has some tricky words in it for any early primary school child, let alone one who was still struggling with English. Usually, I mimed instead of actually singing – particularly those hard songs like the national anthem and Australian bush ballads like Click Go the Shears.

It wasn't until much later, when I could read and was matching up the written words of the anthem with the actual song that I said to myself, "Girt by sea? Was that what I was supposed to be singing?"

Bringing home report cards was always wrought with disappointment in those early years. It was like announcing to the world how far behind I was. Each semester, I handed over the envelope with the report in it and stood there, silent, as my mother read it. Her shoulders would slump. Her lips would press together and her eyes would close. It was as if she was trying to keep all her thoughts inside. She would sigh, then lean over and put her hand on my shoulder. "It's okay, Mona," she'd say each time. "You try hard and that's important. If you keep practising and listening to your teacher, you will be at the top of the class!"

When Dad came home, his reaction was the same. They tried hard not to show their concern but kids are perceptive, and kids listen when you think they're not.

"Have we done the right thing, Aida?" Dad said to Mum. "Bringing them here, to Australia?"

"I don't know. It's hard for them."
They never blamed us. They blamed themselves.

Then, in Year 3, I got Miss Bray. Some teachers just make an impression and she was one of them.

There was nothing extraordinary about her appearance – light brown hair, in her thirties, tall and slim – or about what she taught us. She had a beautiful smile, though, and kind, caring words always came out of her mouth.

The minute I stepped into her classroom, it was like everything just started to click.

Sometimes my writing or spelling was really bad. I knew that. So did she. Yet she patiently explained and corrected my mistakes like I was the only student in the classroom. Then she always made a positive comment. It was the boost I needed at that time and it let me know I was going to be okay.

She was like another mum to me. I truly felt she was genuinely invested in my development, not just doing her job as a teacher.

"I'm getting married," she told us towards the end of the year.

The class went nuts. We were all so happy for her.

In the short space of a year, I went from being a timid reader to reading aloud with confidence and I'd moved to the top of the class in maths. Miss Bray changed my life and set me on a trajectory of lifelong learning and inquiry.

Teachers like this often only come around once in a lifetime. However, I was lucky because I had two.

Mr Phillip didn't come along until I was in high school but the timing was perfect. He was my maths teacher every year for five years. His passion for mathematics was inspiring. He didn't just teach the textbook and the formulas but talked about the history of maths and where the concepts and formulas came from. Maths came alive on his watch. It was real. The way he taught resonated with me.

He was firm, too. Nobody mucked about in Mr Phillip's classes. Nobody spoke out of turn. He held students in fascination and in a little bit of fear because if we looked like we weren't paying attention, a piece of chalk would come right for us, flying through the air like a missile. Mr Phillip commanded attention and he got it.

There were slip-ups, too, even by me.

"Daydreaming, Mona?" he said to me.

I had been. About boys. It was my age. He stared straight at me – forced me to keep eye contact.

"Leave the daydreaming for the playground. Leave it for later. Daydreaming won't get you the results you need."

That's all he said. He didn't even need the chalk. I never lost focus in his class again.

By Year 10, I was topping nearly all my classes. I was Dux of South Sydney High School. It felt good, especially after my slow beginning. It just goes to show what you can achieve with perseverance and a little support in the way of someone else believing in you.

That belief followed me to a new school for my final year. Moving schools for Year 12 wouldn't be a choice I would normally recommend but it had to be done. Let's just say it came about because of sibling bonds. My younger brother looked out for me. I supported him. It's what family does.

"Aunty Mona," my nephew, Hassan's son, said to me, years later. "I saw your name on that board."

I nodded. "It's still there, is it?" It was the Dux board at the school and my name was on it, engraved and painted in gold.

My nephew's face was full of pride. "That's so fantastic," he said, over and over. "So great."

Indeed, it was.

Mona Shindy

'Unlucky'

As I grew up my family became more established and were blessed with the addition of a new baby sister Freda, when I was ten. Her birth brought us all so much joy, especially for me as a big sister who loved playing house and pretending to be a mum!

Things were going pretty smoothly for us until everything changed in the space of one week.

"I don't think I'll go to work today," Dad said. He was still in his pyjamas and his face seemed pale.

That was the first sign for us. Dad was healthy and active. He was a hard worker. He didn't take sickies.

"It's just a sore arm and tight chest," he said. "Probably slept on it the wrong way. I'll be fine." He smiled but his smile was not bright and it didn't reach his eyes like it usually did.

Mum was worried but she tried to hide it. "Off you go to school," she said to us. "Don't miss the bus now."

As far as Mum and Dad were concerned, it was just a normal school day. Business as usual, except for Dad calling in sick to work.

It wasn't until we arrived home, and Dad wasn't there, that we found out he wasn't fine. The pain had become worse and, because of his symptoms, he'd been admitted to hospital.

"They're keeping him overnight," Mum told us when she finally arrived back home. "He'll have some tests and they will give him treatment for the pain."

I think we were dumbfounded. Nobody said anything.

"Oh," Mum added, "you can still keep going to school. It's all just precautionary."

As it turned out, his 'symptoms' and the reason they were keeping him there were due to pneumonia. The treatment involved beating him on the back to release the phlegm in his lungs suffocating him. However, what would we know? We just assumed it was normal procedure and he was getting the appropriate treatment in hospital.

Mum was called back in the next day. Barely twenty-four hours had passed and my father had gone from fit and busy to having suffered a massive heart attack and a stroke.

Hearing Mum repeat the doctor's words will stay with me forever: "Your husband has been very unlucky, Mrs Shindy. We are sorry."

Fit people who are forty-eight don't die from heart attacks. That's what we believed. But a couple of days later, Mum came home from the hospital. "Look at this," she said.

It was a bank slip for withdrawing money. Mum and Dad had a joint account so they both needed to sign the slips. There, next to Mum's neat signature, were Dad's initials, slightly wobbly, then our surname. He'd written *Shindyyyy*. The letter 'y' was there four times instead of one. That was when I knew something was very, very wrong.

"It's okay," Mum said. "Don't be scared. Don't be sad. Everything will be alright." Her words were strong but her face wasn't. Her face was a picture of helplessness and fear and it told us everything we needed to know about Dad's condition.

Hassan tried to reassure us. In my bedroom, which I shared with my little sister, the four of us would meet – like a support group – while Mum was praying. She prayed a lot. Muslims do that but Mum was praying all the time.

"Listen," Hassan said, his fifteen-year-old voice trying to emulate that of the man-of-the-house. "Dad is a strong man. These things happen all the time and people get better all the time. It's not always bad news. There will be rehabilitation. It will be hard but he's still young. He will be alright."

We all looked at each other and we tried to believe this. We were fifteen, fourteen, thirteen and five.

For several days, I resisted visiting Dad. "I have to study for my exam." That was my excuse. Eventually, though, I finished the exam and had no further excuses so I summoned the courage to go in.

Hospitals are stark places. I'd never really thought about it before – not until I was walking through the corridors with my mum, my brothers and my sister. It was your typical hospital. That smell of chemical cleaner, the beeps of monitors and equipment, people being wheeled around in their beds, the rubber knobs scraping up against the wall, the click of heels on laminate floors. We dodged doctors and nurses dressed in white and blue, cleaners hauling around bins on trolleys and visitors walking around with bunches of already wilting flowers and balloons covered in *Get Well* messages. We weren't carrying anything. We walked past room after room of sick people and silently made our way into intensive care where Dad was receiving treatment. There were many beds separated only by thin sheets that nurses and doctors regularly pulled open to gain access and then closed to provide privacy for patients.

At the entrance to the room, I stopped and stared for a moment. There he was, slumped to one side in a wheelchair beside his bed, unable to keep himself upright. My dad. The side of his face and his lip drooped and the words coming out of his mouth were little more than gibberish to my ears. This is not how a child of fourteen expects to see the man who has always been her tower of strength.

A nurse came past at that moment to check on him. "How are we, Mr Shindy?" she said, bright and happy. She checked the drip and the catheter, made some adjustments and scribbled something on the chart.

"The silver people behind you have been keeping me company. They said they would take me out soon," Dad said to her. His words were slow and slurred but intelligible.

My face reddened and I looked down at the floor. I was devastated. There was no one else in the room. He was hallucinating and confused. The stroke and the clot in his brain had turned him into something he wasn't. It had diminished him; made him a mere shadow of himself. A shadow of the father I had been discussing things with and debating with a mere week ago.

All my life, I'd never known Dad to sit still, stagnating in any one activity. He was always on the go, looking for new opportunities and ways to achieve his next goal. Dad wasn't afraid of hard work. He'd started off in a factory, owned a shop and secured employment with the government. Within ten years of arriving in Australia, he had bought two houses. By the time I was in Year 8, he was halfway through a law degree. Yes, he already had a law degree, but it wasn't recognised in Australia. Dad had big dreams and hopes and everything he did was for our family.

This person in front of me – he was not my dad.

I stood there for a couple of minutes. It was awkward, not knowing what to say or do. Then I noticed his attention shift to me. His mouth worked to form his words. "Monameeno, al-ageeba, al-azeema." The warmth in his eyes and his love as he struggled to say the words he so often greeted me with gave me hope.

He recognised me. My father was still there.

He didn't speak a lot while we were there but we stayed, taking turns to hold his hand while he gave each of us a message.

"Look after your mum," he said to Mohamed. "Make sure you look after your mum."

Hassan leaned in close while Dad gave him his message. None of us heard what he said to Hassan but he nodded.

"I love you, Freda. I'm so happy you came to see me."

"I love you, too, Dad," my five-year-old sister replied. "Come home soon."

Mona Shindy

Then it was my turn. I held his hand.

"Stay strong," he said. "Work hard and do well at school." Words he'd said to me many times before but, at this moment they somehow meant more, like they had more purpose.

I pulled a twenty-cent coin from my pocket and placed it in Dad's pyjama pocket, holding my hand over it for a moment. "You'll be alright, Dad," I said. "Use this money to call home when we can't visit."

Walking out was hard. Leaving him, slumped and lonely in that chair. We all felt it and I knew what we were all thinking as we made our way back through the corridors and past all the sick people.

The air bit as we stood out the front of the building and then piled into the taxi – all five of us. Mum sat beside the driver and the four of us squashed in the back. I managed to squeeze my baby sister in one seatbelt with me, despite the driver's initial protest.

"Dad is in a bad way," Mohamed said. His voice was quiet, barely able to break through the grind of the taxi's engine.

Hassan nodded. "Yes, but the hospital will fix him. He'll get better."

"He will," I said.

I'm not sure how we managed to sleep that night but we did. We were teenagers.

❊⋯✿⋯❊⋯✿⋯❊⋯✿⋯❊⋯✿⋯❊⋯✿⋯❊⋯✿⋯❊

"Dad died! Dad died! Dad died!"

It was Hassan. In my bedroom. On my bed. Shaking me. Screaming. "Dad died."

Shattering Identity Bias

Fully awake now, I understood those words.

Then we were all there. All four of us. Huddled on the floor of the living room. Waiting for Mum to come home and tell us it wasn't true.

※※※※※※※※※※※※

Time passed in a bubble of tears and hugs and then Mum was there. Her eyes were red and puffy. Her face drawn. She was a mess. She ran over to us with her arms wide and we drew her into our huddle.

"Ya awlaad, awladna, awladee."

She said this over and over. *Oh, children. Our children. My children.*

We stayed there like that, listening to her tell us everything that had happened.

In the space of one night, we'd been forced to grow up. Life had changed forever.

Mona Shindy

Grown Up Overnight

The next day, Mum sent us all off to school as though nothing had happened. She put us in a taxi and went about trying to find out what to do about organising a burial. It was probably the first time Mum ever thought about school as a suitable form of childcare rather than an institution for learning. Having settled away from the suburbs that attracted large Muslim groupings, as a family, we had been quite separated from the Australian Muslim community. We only went to the mosque to commemorate significant religious events during the year but we had not ever truly been immersed in the whole community culture, nor did we have many Muslim friends. We practised at home. Mum preferred it that way as she was convinced that too close an association would distract us from our studies and may expose us to religious schools of thought that deviated from the principles-based practice of Islam she had grown up with. Migration to Australia had not only introduced my family to many new cultures but also to different interpretations of how Islam should be practised; not all of them resonated completely with my parents.

I spent the day at school, crying sporadically. I am sure my siblings did, too. Some of my peers didn't know what to say or even how to approach me. They kept their distance as they observed my anguish; some even scurried away quickly so as not to have to engage in any way. My closest friends asked straight out, wanting to understand why I was a mess.

"Why are you crying? What happened?" my friend, Sue, enquired with genuine heartfelt concern etched on her face. Sue was of Lebanese descent and we often practised our Arabic skills on each other. Her brother was also in Hassan's year at school and we had gotten to know them well through sport and being invited over for birthday parties. Their parents really liked us and I suspect felt a strong affinity with us as fellow Muslims in a predominantly non-Muslim society.

"My dad died," I said, struggling through tears and a shortness of breath brought on by my uncontrolled emotions.

"Haraam," she said as she threw her arms around me. She was a lot taller than me and as she tucked me in tightly, I felt completely engulfed by a soft warmth that brought me some much-needed comfort.

I would normally have picked her up about the incorrect use of the word Haraam, which relates to things the Quran classifies as prohibited or sinful for Muslims. She was using the word colloquially as a way of saying she was sorry. It really didn't matter what was said. In that moment, her natural inclination to want to comfort me was more than enough to feel very right.

It was not too long into the day that we were collected by the school social worker and driven home. Mum was offered help and the school organised for a range of community support organisations to visit us at home. The Smith Family and The Salvation Army were among the first to arrive.

"I am really sorry for your loss, Mrs Shindy," The Smith Family caseworker said to Mum. "We are here to help. What do you need?"

"We are okay, thank you," Mum replied. "We don't need anything."

I am sure she was too embarrassed to communicate all her worries about paying the bills with nobody working and bringing in money.

"Mrs Shindy, we can bring you some furniture and clothes for the kids if that would help? How about some crockery," the kind Salvation Army officer offered.

Mum was clearly overwhelmed by all the new faces who came knocking at our door. She would ask my brothers and me to sit with her when people came to visit or to accompany her to Centrelink to help make sure she understood all that was required to seek available government support. We missed a fair few days of school after Dad died. There was so much to do and learn. We also needed time just to grieve, be close and to comfort each other as a family. All the Arabic we had practised as children was now proving invaluable as we took on impromptu roles as interpreters.

There were also visits from many of our school teachers and colleagues from Dad's work. You never forget such people. These are the souls that bind society together and restore faith in humanity's goodness.

What Mum did achieve on that first day was to find out that Lakemba Mosque had a burial coordination office and bathing facility attached to it. Such facilities are very important for Muslims as there are specific traditions and practices observed during burials. The body is thoroughly cleansed and wrapped in a simple white shroud before being placed directly into the ground. We arrive on this earth with nothing and return in exactly the same form.

It was a stressful time for Mum. Not only was she mourning and responding to her children's emotional needs but, somehow, she couldn't access any money for quite some time. It was sitting in my father's account and, of course, he could no longer sign to have it withdrawn. My parents never dealt with credit cards and a good portion of the family income was still funding house mortgages.

The next day, we accompanied Mum to Lakemba Mosque. It was a grand building that looked quite out of place among the adjoining residential houses. It had a large dome roof and minarets, similar to the great mosques one might see in a documentary exploring the architecture of the Middle East. Inside, it was quiet and tranquil; a large carpeted hall with intricate Arabic calligraphy and beautiful mosaics on the walls. The community there was marvellous. They wrapped their arms around us, collected funds for the burial plot and body-cleansing activities and worked diligently to secure the early release of Dad's remains from the coroner. It is important in the Islamic faith tradition that a dead person be buried as quickly as possible. Mum was stressing about it for the whole three days it took. There was visible relief on her face and finally an ability to sleep once Dad had been laid to rest.

I was exhausted by this time. Crying, interpreting, listening, learning, documenting, reading, comforting, worrying; it all seemed to go on non-stop with a circular repetition. Amidst the pain came the realisation that if we were to survive as a family, we would all need to contribute. We would all need to lead. I personally no longer needed to be asked to do anything; I was often already doing things well before Mum was aware they needed doing.

In those three days, so much had happened. We had lost a father and gained a community. There was no blood family to carry Dad's coffin. There were no people to call to alert them of the funeral but there were so many hands that carried him and community members that prayed for him. It took my father's death for me to truly understand what Islamic brotherhood and sisterhood are all about. It was the first time in my life that I truly appreciated the importance of community service; of helping those less fortunate and protecting the vulnerable. I had observed my parents give in charity every year, as prescribed in Islamic teachings, but had never observed the community in action, making good use of those funds or selflessly giving of their time, skills and energy to support others. The whole experience had a profound impact on my mindset. I was not only determined to make my father proud by achieving all that he had dreamed for me, but to do so in a way that meant contributing fully to the betterment of all the communities to which I belonged.

My father's death also reinvigorated our focus as a family on our Islamic faith. Mum started wearing a hijab in public and we all began to read the Quran more frequently at home. We were all determined to be better practicing Muslims.

The years that followed were incredibly challenging indeed. I remember scrounging around the house looking for loose change to buy milk; one of many basic commodities that regularly ran out in between strictly budgeted weekly shopping trips.

"Have a look on my side table, Mona. Maybe there are some coins behind the clock radio," Mum said.

"Look underneath the couch cushions. Coins might have fallen out of someone's pockets," Freda added.

We didn't always find money and would then have to do without until the next social security support payment or Dad's superannuation pension came in. Money was very tight but somehow we made things work. I would regularly hide school excursion permission notes from Mum because I didn't want her to worry about not having enough money to send me. I would just tell my teachers that I wasn't allowed to go. I'm sure some interpreted that information as having something to do with 'weird Islamic beliefs' but the more perceptive ones understood the financial challenges we faced.

I remember Mum putting a little money away each week for a couple of months so Mohamed could go to the theatre with his English class to see Macbeth. It was an evening performance at the Capitol Theatre in Sydney and all of Mohamed's classmates were dressed in smart casual attire, appropriate for such an outing. Mohamed was in one of Hassan's old tracksuits that were clearly a little big for him.

"It was really embarrassing. The kids stared at me and my teacher, Mr Burns, looked as though he pitied me," Mohamed told us when he got home. I felt dreadful for him.

The very next day, Mohamed told us over dinner that Mr Burns had organised an opportunity for him to do some paid tutoring. The opportunity was presented as an acknowledgement and reward for Mohamed topping the class in English, but it only made Mohamed, and indeed all of us, more embarrassed about the financial difficulties we had as a family.

Mum was generally against us working during school terms and was very keen to ensure we dedicated a good deal of effort to our studies. We were, however, encouraged to work in the holidays. I remember working in the kitchen of a maternity hospital when I had finished Year 10. I was responsible for handing out the meals to new mums and loading the dishwasher at the end of my shift. I loved that job, particularly when I got glimpses of the newborns. I saved enough money that year to buy a few nice casual outfits that I could wear outside of school. The rest of my earnings went to help with household bills. Hassan and Mohamed did the local paper delivery run and several customer service jobs in retail stores around Christmas time. As older children, we used to love buying things for our baby sister, Freda, whenever we could. In many ways, we took on a large number of parenting responsibilities when it came to her education and entertainment.

Mum used whatever psychological carrots she could dream up to ensure we stayed focused on our school work. For me, she knew the idea of 'Dad being proud of me' was enough to guarantee my commitment.

"Your father would have been so proud of you with these excellent results, Mona. He would have been so happy," she would say. I could also see that my successes brought her great joy; something I reasoned she deserved amidst all the fear, uncertainty and trauma.

Not only did I diligently focus on my school studies but I felt an absolute responsibility to support Mum. I taught myself many things through inquiry, research and initiative. I couldn't bear to see her worry and I knew she stressed a lot when dealing with unfamiliar people and issues Dad would normally have handled. From doing the family tax returns, learning to drive and engaging contractors when needed, to dealing with solicitors, banks and insurance companies to manage family affairs, I took on a lot of responsibility as a teenager. I didn't really have a social life in high school. My life essentially consisted of school lessons, school sport, household responsibilities and study. My recreational activities were limited to weekly episodes of *Friends* and *Home and Away*. The nightly news and the political program, Sunday, were my primary links to the events and debates raging in the world around me.

My mother endured so much in her life, with my father's death being only one of many challenges she had in raising four children. As with most families, the challenges, setbacks and disappointments were many but she persisted. She raised two engineers and two lawyers. She cared for her grandchildren when they were young and we left for work. She gave us everything, often at the expense of her own comfort and needs. Her selfless example and unconditional love truly inspired me and taught me what the strong bonds of family can produce, even in the most arduous and frightening of circumstances. She taught me about the influence one person can have in supporting the success of others. She taught me about the joy and immense satisfaction gained from giving.

Having lived frugally for so long, I was very motivated at university to secure a cadetship that would help fund my electrical engineering studies and place me on a secure career path. I applied to Telecom initially and was successful in securing a position that would cover my study costs and pay me a modest allowance. Hassan had joined the navy via an undergraduate cadetship program. It was not long before the postcards he was sending home and his tales of adventure in foreign lands had me wondering if I should also try to join the navy. He vividly described navigating big bustling cities in the USA, swimming amongst colourful coral in the Great Barrier Reef and tasting exotic street foods in Asia. It sounded and looked fantastic. We hadn't travelled for years since Dad died.

The navy was paying more than Telecom and that black winter uniform with its sharp and stylish jacket was more than enough reason for me, an impressionable twenty-year-old, to want to explore the option. The opportunity to do something important and admirable as part of a critical national institution was an afterthought, but still very relevant to my final decision to join.

Chapter 2
The Early Career

Leadership and Adventure

*"*It is my pleasure to inform you that you have been successful through the recruitment process and highly recommended for a commission." These words ushered in what would turn out to be a good part of my working life and identity. "Welcome to the team, Ma'am."

So began the indoctrination into my new world with its unique language, culture and traditions.

Two years into my electrical engineering degree at the University of NSW and there I was, getting fitted out for Navy uniforms. A few weeks earlier, I had attended an Officer Selection Board after successfully navigating the prerequisite aptitude tests.

I was really excited. I had hit a point in my studies where I was losing motivation. Each day seemed to drag on with a seemingly never-ending injection of complex engineering concepts and calculations. Securing the Navy Cadetship gave me something amazing to look forward to. It helped me refocus and tackle my studies with a newfound determination to get through. The promise of adventure and travel at the end of my degree was something valuable to strive for.

"Congratulations *habebti (my love)*," Mum said when she heard I had been successful in joining the navy. At that stage, just like me, she had no specific ideas about how my career experience or trajectory would pan out. She was just happy that I was happy. All we both really knew was that I would get to work with advanced technologies and have opportunities for travel and adventure. After Dad died, Mum had instinctively started to shield us from too much interaction with a few Muslim community members who stepped in to help and support us. She was uncomfortable with some of the advice they were giving my brothers about skipping higher-level education to start working straight away. She didn't like that I was receiving marriage proposals at such a young age. She began to quarantine us from what she considered restrictive and limiting stereotyped thinking about gender and societal roles. She understood, from the comments she had heard relating to Hassan joining the navy – "What for? They kill Muslims" – that the Muslim community's reactions to me following a similar path would be even more judgemental.

All of a sudden, I felt a little important. I was only twenty and people much older than me were now referring to me as 'Ma'am'. It was really strange receiving what appeared to be instant respect from unfamiliar people who were quite clearly more experienced and knowledgable about the navy than I was. I felt like I should be giving them that respect, if not only because of our age difference. I trod lightly as I went and, over time, worked out how to best strike the right balance in exercising rank and positional authority while at the same time respecting and honouring the specialist skillsets of the many highly capable and dedicated people who worked for me during my career.

I would be sent to various Navy bases during university breaks. These included training establishments, dockyards and city offices housing support organisations that helped keep our ships and people at sea.

Initially, I completed a short course at HMAS *Creswell* that familiarised me with Navy procedures, the etiquette for being an officer and the building blocks needed for 'being a leader and officer first and an engineer second'. The course ran for two weeks and was comprised of a group of undergraduates just like myself. They came from all corners of Australia and were studying a range of different degrees. Navy called us Supplementary List Officers as we were extras to the recruits who either joined directly from school or studied at the Australian Defence Force Academy.

That first course ran early in the new year, between my third and fourth year of university. Perfect summer weather and white sandy beaches on the base provided a deceptively beautiful backdrop to the serious business of developing Australia's future military leaders. We were introduced to the basics of life in the Royal Australian Navy as we admired majestic gumtrees and mobs of kangaroos that fearlessly cut off our marching squads as we traversed on the immaculately-kept lawns. It was the first time I had lived in communal quarters with people other than family. We were issued even more uniforms and taught how and when to wear them in different settings. We pretended our accommodation building was a ship and were expected to look after it as our home. I was keen to build strong friendships and willingly contributed to all activities, helped others and did a whole lot of cleaning of the common areas, including the showers and toilets. It wasn't long before I realised we, as a cohort of cadets, were also being assessed by the training staff in relation to our leadership qualities. Our behaviours were being scrutinised at every turn. Soon *influence* and *persuasion* became just as important as doing and supporting. We were taught about naval history and how to perform traditional ceremonies for the raising and lowering of the Australian Naval Ensign each day.

I felt very proud and privileged to be part of the Australian Defence Force. I loved it! I loved the discipline, the professionalism and the idea of making a difference in the lives of those in my charge as well as through my contribution to the nation.

After university, HMAS *Creswell* again became the setting for more in-depth training and preparation for life at sea, national representative duties and leadership. We were taught everything, including how to use cutlery properly and dine with others.

"You start using the set cutlery from the outside and then work your way in with each new course," the instructing steward advised.

"Never start eating before the most senior person at the table begins."

"It is polite not to scoff everything on your plate and to place your knife and fork side-by-side to indicate you have finished eating."

From there, the lessons came thick and fast. We learned how to lead others, how to march and understand Defence rank structures, the 'rules of the road', how to navigate at sea and how to care for and emotionally support our sailors. We were also taught how to live in close proximity to others and function efficiently as members of teams.

"If one member of your squad has a poorly ironed uniform, you all get an extra hour of drill!" the Gunnery Officer barked.

"The heads are filthy so no one gets to step ashore until the mess decks are spotless," our Divisional Officers would proclaim. Once we understood the 'heads' referred to the toilets, 'stepping ashore' meant leaving the naval base and the 'mess decks' referred to our accommodation blocks, we quickly harmonised our activities and better supported each other in order to improve our lives.

It was at this time I first realised how much was expected of us as officers. This was no usual job. I was now part of the profession of arms, a lethal warfighter sworn to protect Australia and its interests, a leader, engineer, social worker and national representative. It was a vocation; a way of life I soon fell head over heels in love with.

I guess I initially appreciated the routines and structure. There was something mathematical and logical about it – if you do these things, you will realise these rewards. The routines and regular pay brought a degree of certainty that had been missing in my life. As an officer, I was acknowledged as responsible and capable of making important decisions that would set trajectories for the organisation and those who served in my charge. I felt like I belonged and was trusted to help design and nurture the future Navy while protecting the safety of the broader Australian community. I had been asked to represent my nation. I was welcomed into a revered and respected Australian family. The trainers told me that I was equal to my peers and treated me as though I was deserving of inclusion and mateship. I felt respected and loved. Perhaps for the first time in my life, I was honoured and proud to feel completely Australian.

Despite all my excitement, it was my first time away from home and I missed my family immensely. I worried about how Mum was coping with both Hassan and me away. I knew Mohamed would be doing his best to support Mum and Freda but he, of course, had his own challenges trying to finish a law degree and dealing with an intense sense of loss after Dad passed. There were many days I felt guilty about not being present, if not just to provide emotional support.

We did manage to keep things moving forward despite the separation. Freda was key to the family's success in this regard. She wrote every week to update Hassan and me on events at home and also waited for hours trying to get through by phone. We didn't have mobile phones back then, at least not with the mainstream population. HMAS *Creswell* had one public phone booth, which had to serve about two hundred cadets, so finding it unoccupied between classes was very difficult. We also had one incoming phone line on each floor of the accommodation quarters. This had to service about thirty cadets. I am sure Freda continued ringing right up to lights out at 2200 hours to get a free line between the endless back-to-back conversations cadets were engaged in after normal training hours. Mum, Mohamed and Freda always communicated that things were fine; they worried just as much about Hassan and me as we did about them. The world could be collapsing but nothing was ever said that might shift my focus from my new work obligations.

After the initial period of training when we were confined to the base, I took every opportunity to get home. I would generally leave as soon as I could on a Friday afternoon and return as late as possible on Monday morning. Often, I left Sydney before 4 am on Mondays, dodging kangaroos and navigating tight and bendy roads through the national park, to get to the base just south of Nowra before early morning activities, which regularly involved running on the beach from 6 am. After listening to 80s pop music on full pelt for two hours, I would arrive, fully awake and energised, ready to tackle the soft white sands of Captain's Beach and the often damp rainforest tracks on what was one of three five-kilometre fitness runs per week. I couldn't risk being late and would always dress in my sports uniform before I left Sydney; regularly only having a minute or two to spare after parking my car and charging to the muster point. One particular morning, I remember being about ten minutes late after sleeping in because I'd stayed up too late watching movies with Freda.

"You okay to run, Sub-Lieutenant Shindy?" the physical training instructor greeted me as I approached. It took me a minute to register that he apparently knew something I didn't. "Williams told me you seemed unwell last night."

"I think I'm okay to try," I replied, careful not to acknowledge or confirm the non-existent illness being referred to. The last thing I wanted to do was to incriminate Williams!

"That's the spirit! That's what I want to hear! I'm impressed you've pushed yourself to be here with your division."

In that instant, I was no longer going to be in trouble for being late but was being celebrated as a committed, team-oriented champion. This was one of many incidents that would follow where the strong team bonds being built would carry me and the entire cohort through the most difficult of circumstances.

Despite the close bond I had with home, it was not long before my Navy cohort became my second family. It is just the nature of life in the military. Living in tight quarters, thrown together as teams through arduous challenges and helping each other get through – you can't help but see the humanity and vulnerability in those around you, all while coming to terms with your own strengths and weaknesses. Coupled with the training regime seeking to align team values and goals, it didn't take long for me to form strong friendships with people that I knew I would care for forever. Apart from Williams, who actually ended up deciding the military wasn't for her before we finished our initial training, there were engineers Baston and Wright, who followed a career trajectory similar to mine, and Seaman Officer Huxtable, who was appointed Passing Out Parade Commander for our cohort before embarking on a truly impressive and lengthy career in Navy. These are some of the more memorable people and there are too many others to mention, but it would be fair to say I admired them all.

That same environment that was geared to bond people also had unique challenges. At one point, I was sure almost everyone was in some sort of a relationship with someone else. Fraternisation was prohibited, of course, but many seemed to find ways to hook up. There was whispering and giggling in the many cabins that lined the corridors of the accommodation blocks, romantic interludes on the beach in the early morning or late evening and stories of weekend rendezvous off the base. Young adults under training pressure and away from home often found comfort in the friendship of others. Ironically, the deliberate agenda to strengthen teams sometimes ignited romantic connections; relationships that were both short-lived and life-enduring.

It was also the first time I had been exposed to a drinking culture. The concept of 'working hard and playing hard' became an idea that many took to heart. It was important to me that I did things with my colleagues. I wanted to fit in and be accepted, and I also knew that a failure to do so would be career-limiting. On many a weeknight, I ended up at dinner and drinks at the Huskisson Hotel with members of my cohort. It always started out pretty civilly and I enjoyed spending time with my friends and reflecting on the day's activities or new gossip someone was throwing around. Not participating would have meant missing out on understanding the deeper issues, views and challenges; it would have meant not being part of the group's heartbeat. I thoroughly enjoyed these times, right up until the point behaviours started getting a bit risky or conversations became a little too fresh. I was a very sought-after 'duty driver' and while I made a conscious effort to do everything with the others, from going to pubs and clubs to dining out whenever we got the chance, I would only ever stay until the point alcohol-related behaviours started to kick in.

In terms of cultural values, everyone seemed very different to me. I might be praying in my cabin while others were drinking in the mess. Or I might be fasting during Ramadan and struggling with physical activities, due to low energy levels, during major competitions where the tempo was unrelenting. Although the instructors and trainees knew I was fasting – because I'd either told them or they'd noticed I wasn't present at mealtimes – they could never really understand how physically drained I could become. Not having ever experienced a Muslim fasting day or the cumulative effects of several days in a row, it would have been hard for others to relate. I'm sure some thought I was either lying or insane for not drinking water during some of the strenuous exercises we had to complete under the hot Aussie sun.

I was blending different worlds, learning about others and sharing aspects of myself. I could sense people didn't know exactly what to make of me but I also felt very accepted and included. So much so, in fact, that despite the very clear signals I projected, I still got propositioned more times than I care to remember.

"I've grown really fond of you over the last few weeks, Mona. Can I take you out to dinner?"

"I know you're not the type who has short flings or anything like that, but I'm serious about wanting to explore the possibility of a long-term relationship. Would it be okay for us to hang out together?"

I would always reply that I was flattered, then I'd acknowledge their good qualities but say I just wanted to concentrate on my training. There were some who tried to convince me it would all be possible. Their faces and demeanour showed their disappointment. I knew they talked about me amongst themselves and they must have worked out pretty quickly there was no hope with me.

Maybe it was the small proportion of women in the cohort or the isolation of the training environment with many far away from home but the approaches were many and, in the main, respectfully genuine. I knew myself to be forthright and firm but was shocked, some thirty years later, when my son told me his boss, a colleague from my intake, remembered only one thing clearly about me; that being my words: "I'm sorry. Please don't take offence, but I'm not going to marry anyone other than a Muslim." I didn't want people wasting their energy, nor was a bit of hanky panky ever going to be on the cards. My upbringing had me place incredible importance on the depth of relationships, the importance of Islam in the home and the value of the institution of marriage. When I reflect on my words now, I can understand how my beliefs and behaviours are just as responsible for keeping me distant from colleagues as are any of their beliefs or attitudes towards me.

There was one Sunday afternoon, however, when things got more than a little out of control. I was heading back to my cabin from the common laundry after having ironed some uniforms for the week ahead. Three guys from my division were returning from what sounded like a great day out. They had been drinking and were in a loud and happy mood. Spotting me in the corridor, one grabbed me in a big bear hug, picked me up and swung me around. It was awkward and very sexual with his chest pressed hard against my breasts. He was telling me he loved me, which wasn't all that surprising given that a week earlier he had cornered me for a deep and meaningful conversation about him being prepared to convert to Islam "if I would have him".

Mona Shindy

I asked him to put me down and said something about having been over this with him before. Religion requires a genuine personal belief and commitment and should never be a means to an end.

I went into my cabin and started to lay my uniform out on my bed. Before I'd finished, I found myself face down with my head pushed into the sheets and mattress, and a body on top of me, holding me down.

"I know you want it," a voice said – not the one who'd just bear-hugged me, but one of his mates.

Heart racing, I somehow pushed him off me. Drunk and pants undone, he staggered and I managed to shove him out the door. Laughter erupted. They were all there, watching on.

Like a child trying to escape from the bogeyman, I slammed the door and twisted the lock as fast as I could.

Despite feeling almost superhuman moments ago, I dropped to the floor and sat, too afraid to move, riding out the continuous knocking, mocking laughter and occasional pounding on the door.

Eventually, after what seemed like an eternity, they left.

I didn't go to dinner that night and only surfaced for classes the next day where there would be safety in numbers. People knew what had happened – I heard the chatter and saw the glances – but nobody reported it.

Neither did I.

I have never hidden my religious beliefs from my work colleagues. Nor have I actively thrust them on anyone. For me, religion is personal and my approach is only to share if asked to do so. Islam does, however, guide my life choices and, as such, allows people to quickly identify me as a little different to the majority, particularly within the still very homogenous circles of the Australian Defence Force.

Another memorable and equally confronting incident that occurred at the Naval College and highlighted my differences from the majority happened during a dinner with a senior officer on the base.

We had been invited to his home as part of our training. It was important that we could demonstrate how to eat properly with knives and forks and to hold a pleasant conversation with dignitaries. Finally, we were taught the etiquette of giving thanks through the writing of letters to senior officers and their wives after being hosted in their homes. The night was going very well with each of us diligently adhering to protocol, waiting for the most senior at the table to eat first before we started, using the correct cutlery for the various courses and filling the silence with small talk.

The hosting officer then somehow shifted the dialogue to a discussion on 'Islam and the evil terrorist threat' that it presented. I was gobsmacked. An Australian Naval Officer, a senior member of the training establishment, my boss, someone I was meant to aspire to be like, had completely rubbished my faith and in turn, rubbished me in a few short sentences in front of my peers. I felt very uncomfortable and remained withdrawn for the rest of the evening while my colleagues in the room each glanced at me, almost apologetically, from time to time.

Again, no one said anything. Again, neither did I.

There is so much goodness and strength in Navy culture but there are also weaknesses in the hierarchical structure that deters any challenging of a senior person's ideas and beliefs. I wondered about the institution I had joined and reflected on whether I had made the right choice or, in fact, if I would endure. At this stage, the only Muslims I knew of in the navy were my brother and myself. We were both so junior, having little or no influence or ability to sway the ideas of the senior majority who still looked and thought in a very uniformly different way to us.

Despondent, I was comforted by my friends back in the accommodation blocks. "He would be highly embarrassed if he knew you were Muslim," they told me.

I didn't want him to be embarrassed. I wanted him to be speaking from a position of knowledge and fairness; one informed by knowing Muslims and understanding what motivates and drives them. It was not what he was talking about that evening. It certainly wasn't about the mainstream Islamic community. I knew then that my presence in the Australian Navy would at least serve to educate others; hopefully making it easier for me and any children I might have in the future.

I did well at the college and was identified early as exhibiting strong leadership skills. They had split us up into divisions comprised of those we lived with in the different accommodation blocks on the base. I was in Cook Division and given the honour to lead my squad during the Passing Out Parade that would signify the completion of our officer training. We had practised for weeks. On the day of the parade, the cohort were all very polished. The uniforms were in pristine condition; washed and ironed, with litres of starch impregnating each crease to ensure they remained laser-sharp throughout the proceedings.

My younger brother, Mohamed, had driven my mother down for the parade. She spent the first part of the day marvelling at the beauty of HMAS *Creswell*. 'Booderee', the name of the national park in which the base is nestled, means 'Bay of Plenty' in the local Yuin people's language. We had been given a couple of hours off in the morning to show our guests around. The crystal clear turquoise waters of Jervis Bay and the abundant kangaroo colonies that cohabited the naval base were unfamiliar sites that gave her the sense that she was somewhere very special. She also couldn't stop looking at me and smiling. She didn't say much, nor did she have to as her eyes did more than enough to communicate the depth of her love and the immense pride she felt to see her baby all grown up and independent. An engineer and an Australian Naval Officer; not a doctor but a very acceptable alternative in her view. Every Egyptian parent I knew and many of those from other migrant backgrounds had a thing about wanting their kids to be doctors. I was delighted that Mum was happy. I hadn't seen her beaming for years; not since Dad died.

It was soon time for the formal proceedings. I headed off to find my squad as the families were ushered to the viewing stands. The parade commenced with the pounding of drums, music and the barking of orders. I was positioned in front of my squad, comprised of approximately twenty cadets. On either side, there were three similar-sized squads with a Parade Commander standing in front of all of us on the grassed quarterdeck facing the senior dignitaries. The parade band, a group of highly skilled and talented professional military musicians, had positioned themselves off to the side of the parade ground. I knew the circuit very well and had mastered exactly when to call out orders to steer and control the squad that followed behind me.

"Cook Division. Into line. Right turn!" I shouted at the top of my lungs. It was hard to project my voice above the music of the band. Instructions were sequenced with marching steps against the backdrop of a meticulously marked out ground. We moved in unison. I was immensely proud of the whole cohort; not to mention myself for making it to this point. I thought we were all very polished, accurately portraying the fruits of the hard yards we had just completed. I felt we were well trained, professional and ready to do our families, Navy and nation proud.

After being inspected by the Chief of the Defence Force, it was time for each squad to do a final lap of the ground, march past and salute the inspecting officer who had now positioned himself on a podium, behind which all invited family and friends were seated.

Mona Shindy

I was intensely focused on getting my timing correct so my squad and I would turn our heads to the right at the exact moment necessary to ensure we correctly saluted the Chief of the Defence Force as we passed the podium. As my squad approached the podium, my mind turned to sequencing my orders to the march steps.

"Cook Division, eyes right!" I ordered, my words in time with the squad's right footsteps.

It went off without a hitch, eyes aligned with those of the Chief of the Defence Force, and a salute sharply delivered and reciprocated in kind.

It was not long before my serious and focused expression melted away and was replaced by a wide smile. At that moment, the intensity of my discipline and determination for precision was drowned out by strong feelings of warmth and joy. I had only held the Chief's gaze for less than a second before I noticed my mum behind him. She was standing in the stands. Her hijab was fluttering in the wind and she was jumping up and down as she clapped. If anyone had missed her before, they most certainly would be aware of her presence now. She was literally the only person on her feet in the stands. Freda was pulling on her skirt to try to get her to sit but Mum didn't care about what others might have been thinking. She looked completely lost in the moment and singularly did more than enough to communicate how all the parents present must have felt as they watched her with broad smiles, but too embarrassed to copy.

I guided my squad members around the parade ground to bring them to a final position, aligned with the other squads. We all faced the podium in preparation for the helicopter flyover, which would signal the finalisation of proceedings. As helicopters from the nearby HMAS *Albatross* flew low and loud over the parade, I could feel my heart thump hard against the air pressure they generated. With the delight of success and immense pride, I joined my graduating class as we grabbed our hats and threw them high in the air.

I was now a fully trained and competent naval officer – ready to deploy to sea.

Mona Shindy

Posted to Sea

After completing an extra six months of technical and navy equipment training at HMAS *Cerberus* in southern Victoria, I joined HMAS *Canberra*, an Adelaide Class frigate, and was posted to sea.

It sounds strange, but I hadn't thought deeply about actually 'going to sea' when I joined the navy. The recruiters had said things like: "There's a variety of career paths as an engineer, like shore communications, for example." I suppose I'd developed the idea, from this, that going to sea was not mandatory. Initially, of course, I'd been excited at the potential for travel to exotic locations like those my brother had seen with the navy. However, as I got closer to the prospect of potential deployment to sea, the idea of separation from family became a reality and I started to have second thoughts. I worried about Mum and my younger siblings and wondered how they would fare with both myself and Hassan away.

It was too late though, misgivings or not. I had a return of service obligation of three years because the Navy had paid all my expenses during my final two years of university.

HMAS *Canberra* was off to join a Rim of the Pacific (RIMPAC) exercise off the USA coast, with some great port visits planned for Hawaii and San Diego along the way. I had an 'engineering journal' and a ship 'Officer of the Day' task book to complete before I could sit a written examination and board associated with each one at the end of my posting. Although I was apprehensive at the thought of leaving my family, my excitement soon returned at the prospect of what was before me and I was determined to remain open-minded and enthusiastic to learn and grow through every activity I was involved in.

Amongst a crew of two hundred and twenty, I was one of only three women – a female Sub-Lieutenant logistician under training, the ship's doctor (a Lieutenant) and myself, a Sub-Lieutenant weapons electrical engineer under training. It was in the early 1990s and the navy had only just begun to integrate women into ships that would see active service. Our ship, one of Navy's premier warships at the time, had never carried women before. The sailors guarding the gangway leered and smirked as I boarded the ship. "Oooh, check it out," they called. I ignored them and saluted the white ensign.

I don't remember having any conversations about this type of behaviour with the other two ladies. It just wasn't something we talked about. Even though we shared accommodation, we were in separate departments and our days were spent predominantly working in different compartments. Each of us was closer to and more involved with the sailors in our own team and we would often only see each other as we rushed to get ready in the morning or as we went to sleep at night.

The three of us were housed in a cramped three-berth cabin that had been hastily converted from its previous life as a boat locker. A tiny sink was positioned next to the bunk racks, one above the other. With less than two square metres of standing room, we had to store all our possessions in small compartments beneath each of our racks. Suffice to say, once our uniforms were secured, there was not much room for anything else. I carried the bare minimum in terms of personal effects and only had a few outfits I could mix and match if I was stepping ashore.

I soon met the head of the Weapons Electrical Engineering Department. My new boss was welcoming and very clear about his expectations. He outlined the upcoming program for the ship and explained that it offered a great opportunity for me to see all the weapons systems in action. This would provide the perfect way for me to finalise my engineering journal and Officer of the Day task book.

"Get involved," he said, "and ask lots of questions. The team will help you learn about the systems you need to understand." He then allocated me to one of the young sailors in the department. "Show Sub-Lieutenant Shindy around and introduce her to the others."

The first few days at sea were very hectic as I learned the ship's routines, its layout and important procedures I would need to follow in case of emergency. The sailors were generally friendly when I engaged directly with them. They offered up information, explained the duties they performed and the operations of the systems they maintained.

I found it strange how connected everyone was. Sound-powered phones throughout the ship were an incredibly effective means of relaying messages between compartments. In fact, I know how useful they were as the sailors seemed very informed as I moved from one ship compartment to the next.

They were well briefed on where I had been and who I had spoken with before I even showed up to speak to them. At times, it felt like everyone was talking about me and knew my exact movements. It was as if I was an enigma – the subject of debate and analysis – scored and rated against the other two women on the ship.

The nature of the environment only became truly apparent to me when I first sat down with my boss to review my engineering journal entries and sign off on my progress. I had put a lot of effort into providing fulsome answers to the questions asked. I explained in detail the operations of the ship's sensors and effectors. From the radars to the missile launch system, I knew it all. At least, that's what I thought.

"How did you get those answers?" he asked. His smile broadened as he continued to read. It was not long before he could no longer control his laughter.

Laughter! I was horrified. Embarrassed. Why was he laughing at me?

"Those answers are ..." He paused. "... incorrect. Actually, some of them are even ludicrous." He looked at me, still laughing. "I think the crew have been taking the piss."

It was Navy tradition, apparently. All those hours I'd spent 'consulting' and 'learning', the weapons engineering department had been doing nothing more than making a mockery of me for their own entertainment. I couldn't believe it. This is when it really hit home that, as a female, the odds were stacked against me and I knew I would have to work much harder than my male peers to get ahead. I found the whole situation very frustrating and upsetting. It made me feel like an outsider, unappreciated and unwanted. There were many times I felt as though I just wanted to quit.

I didn't know who to trust anymore. Complex equipment maintenance and user manuals became my mode of learning late at night. In my mind, this was preferable to being 'taught' by the crew. I was determined to get through my training successfully and worked extra long and hard. I resented that though, as it was made unnecessarily difficult for no good reason. Just like everyone else, I needed time for rest and fun; something I feel I did not get enough of.

Even though the boss did speak to the department and general behaviour did improve over time, there were many who simply could not help themselves and my name appeared many times in the 'Stiff Shit' books littered around the ship. Back then, the navy had, and still has in many ways today, a way of breaking people down and building them up again through well-worn training and indoctrination practices.

Shared experiences helped build community and culture; a common understanding of expected and acceptable behaviour. Differences of any kind, however, often became points of focus and ridicule. Nobody was immune.

These 'Stiff Shit' books, should they be found today, would give great insights into a culture that isolated and made fun of those who did not fit the majority mould. To put it simply, these books were repositories where sailors would pen the details of pranks they played on others. They would document the embarrassment of the victim and each story finished with the words 'Stiff Shit!' – the mark of achievement and victory. Given that women were very much in the minority, we all featured very heavily in these books, alongside some of the male crew who exhibited any noticeable differences in cultural views or behaviour.

Prior to our big deployment to the USA, the ship had been running weekly out of Sydney. We had been training and working in preparation for the war game exercises ahead of us. Early on in my posting, I was able to go home for a few weekends. At the time, Hassan had been away, posted to a destroyer escort homeported in Western Australia. It was the time of the first Gulf War and Mum told me Hassan was also experiencing a rough time on his ship.

'Hussein' they called him. It was a play on his name, drawing a comparison between him and the national enemy and dictator, Saddam Hussein. 'Arab' was another nickname they'd given him and he was mocked as a 'likely enemy within'.

"He tries to laugh it off," Mum said, "and pretend it doesn't affect him." She was really worried for Hassan. It upset her that he was isolated among people who made him feel different; like an outsider not to be trusted. The social worker in her would have understood the psychological impact the smart comments had on him. Her face said it all, crunched forehead and downturned lips.

Friendly banter – that's what they would have called it. Like me, Hassan went along with it, too. "I just played along," he said much later. " 'Yes, I could be a sleeper. I might be activated when you least expect it!' That's what I'd say." Hassan was alone across the other side of the country and did not get too many opportunities to come home and decompress. Mum was wonderful at supporting her children emotionally, however, in an era where email and mobile phones had yet to take hold, connecting with her was often very difficult.

I felt bad for Hassan because I knew he was suffering. In the Navy of the early 90s, not drinking with the boys was another sure-fire way to get ostracised. I didn't drink either but for me, as a woman, I could get away with it more easily. There was something sophisticated, refined and feminine about women who refrained and many found that attractive.

Ultimately, Hassan only served for six years and retired as a Lieutenant. When he left, he had nearly been broken in the process of pursuing a 'redress of grievance' where he was seeking remedy for the poor and discriminatory practices to which he had been subjected. He experienced a culture of 'gang ups' and the 'closing of ranks', which was aimed more at 'weeding out' rather than holding the mainstream to account.

Hassan was accused of being lazy and not working hard enough to get things done, but it is somewhat difficult when others are actively sabotaging your efforts. It was a system hell-bent on blaming the different individual, rather than examining itself in relation to its preparedness to absorb and accept that individual. He resigned for his own sanity. At the time, he felt so let down and downtrodden that he was not sleeping well. He wanted to get as far away as he could from those who had not accepted him; so much so that he did not even stay on as a Reserve Officer. He felt he needed to sever all ties.

Hassan's experiences made me angry and I quickly formed the view that I should look for alternate career opportunities outside Defence, once I finished my return of service obligation. Life in the fleet seemed very different from what the training at HMAS *Creswell* had promised. The professionalism and discipline seemed lacking. The difficulty Hassan experienced in getting the shortfalls seriously addressed, made me question if any further investment of my time was justified.

Mona Shindy

Fitting In

I experienced a great deal of loneliness during that first deployment.

My sister kept all the letters I sent home.

I hate my life, Freed! The sailors are always telling me wrong things and I feel like I am falling way behind on finishing my task book. I can't stand the fact that I have to read long complex chapters of technical manuals just to get some understanding of what the onboard equipment does. It shouldn't be that hard.

I can't stand the vulgarity of the environment. Naked pictures everywhere and someone is always 'spruiking on' about their last conquest. I lost it today in the wardroom. You can't even just sit and relax in the only recreational space allocated to the officers. I had just walked in after a really long day running around with the sailors doing maintenance on the gear.

"Get us a coffee, Sub!" was the remark I heard, barely one metre into the compartment. Amongst the laughter that followed, I came back with "Get it yourself, Sir," before turning around and getting right out of there, and slamming the door on my way.

I'll probably get some restriction of privileges for disobeying an order. I don't care anymore. I've had enough. Some of these guys are just out of control!

I also got really seasick as soon as the ship sailed this morning. It's a recurring theme for me. I want to throw up all the time. I have to take seasickness tablets just to keep upright. I want to come home, now. I miss you a lot.

Got your letter yesterday. Thanks for thinking of me and writing. I love receiving your notes. Really proud that you did so well on your last English exam. Keep up the great work. I hope Mum is doing okay and Bida is getting through his studies well. If you need anything, just let me know.

Reading them now, I'm amazed I survived.

I was a Sub-Lieutenant under training; the bottom of the heap. There was no real role for me on the ship other than to learn. I was given a couple of collateral duties, including acting as the Liaison Officer for one of the planned Hawaiian ports. My role was to prepare a visitor's manual for the crew, advising places to visit and activities to do while we were in port. Of course, a key part of the document was 'good places to drink'.

I was also assigned to be the ship's 'video officer'. A tricky role, I had to order and return VCR cassettes from port to port, ensuring the ship's company had a movie to watch each night after dinner.

I persevered with the training and, over time, became a well-liked team member. "You're a good sport," I was told, more than once – probably because I refused to let myself get too worked up about some of the highly inappropriate behaviours many of the crew members tried on. What was the point?

The propositions I had become used to continued. It was a male-dominated environment – not that this is an excuse, but I had watched too many of my female colleagues come off badly when they made complaints.

In fact, the first one came right at the beginning of the deployment, on our way to Hawaii before we'd even made it to the equator. I was up on the mainmast of the ship, apparently learning about the ship's communication systems with a Chief Petty Officer.

"I love you," he said.

It was awkward but I dealt with it the same way I dealt with the others – politely and tactfully shutting down the conversation. I could have pulled rank and reported him but my senses all told me that would make things more difficult for me than if I got on with my life and avoided him for a while. I suppose I just wanted to make it through the deployment successfully and complete my initial training.

My ability to diffuse confrontation and uncomfortable situations was something I learned and refined during my early years in the navy. Working around all the boundaries that continued to be crossed, time and time again, had become part of my life. It was something I just did.

A more practical and pressing issue I faced during those first few weeks at sea was the 'disappearance' of my bras and undies. Were they being lost during the washing process? Surely they weren't being taken by the stewards who cleaned my cabin each day? It wasn't just the occasional item either. In fact, I was down to two bras and two pairs of undies by the time we hit our first port in Hawaii, where I could go shopping.

Not long after the mysterious disappearance, I was completing a set of rounds in the technical junior sailors' mess one evening when I noticed one of my pairs of undies hanging on a locker. They were covering the 'private parts' of a topless woman on a poster. Then, I saw one of my bras being used as a clothesline to hold a few towels as they dried in the musky, smelly and damp environment of the mess.

Once again, I did nothing.

What could I have done?

I ignored it and went about my duties knowing there were bigger things to get worked up about than my underwear.

As with many institutions, the navy had its traditions. One of these was the 'Crossing the Line Ceremony', traditionally held on the occasion of the ship crossing the equator. It was like an initiation ceremony for crew members – like myself – who had never crossed the equator on a naval ship before.

I had heard about this ceremony. It involved a crew member dressed up as King Neptune and all sorts of messy concoctions prepared by various other crew members from food scraps. It was all supposed to be 'a bit of fun', with new crew members having to ask Neptune's permission to cross.

It was also an event that could easily get out of control.

On the day of the 'crossing', I had done well for the vast majority of the day to avoid the shipmates who were running the ceremony. It was in this state of avoidance, curled up and hiding in one of the ship's helicopters secured in the hangar, that I finally heard my name being called over the ship's main broadcasting system.

"Where is Sub-Lieutenant Shindy? You might as well show yourself. No-one disrespects and avoids King Neptune!"

There was no way I would be spared from experiencing a hazing. I was one of three 'novelty' females on board so how could I expect to be spared from experiencing the process countless others had endured before me? I was, after all, part of the crew, so I decided to have a bit of fun, play along and create some drama everyone would remember and enjoy for some time.

Sure enough, it wasn't long before they found me in the helicopter. My captors pulled me to the flight deck while I screamed at the top of my lungs. The crew were merciless, hurling eggs and smothering my hair with flour and rotting kitchen waste.

It was all still a bit of fun as someone tied my hands behind my back and lowered me to my knees before the mighty King.

"Please, King Neptune," I begged, "may I be granted permission to cross?"

'King Neptune' was a large and hairy man who was no doubt purposely selected for those traits. All he had on was a crown and speedos and he sat, legs spread, on a makeshift throne. As I kneeled before him, someone placed their hand firmly around my neck from behind and this is where I knew things were about to turn ugly.

I struggled to hold my head back as I was forced, multiple times, face-first into King Neptune's genitals. I was being assaulted but each time I was pushed forward, the crew on the flight deck roared with delight. I couldn't move. I felt helpless.

Eventually, after what seemed like forever, I felt someone push away the hand holding my neck and I was allowed to get up.

Head down, I quickly scurried away.

We still had several days left at sea, meaning water restrictions were necessary as the reverse osmosis plants could only generate a limited amount of fresh water per day. I managed to fill a bucket and sat, brushing the now coagulated flour from my hair before carefully cleaning the crevasses of my body with the little water I had.

Anger and humiliation at what had just happened coursed through my body. There I was, a young lady raised with conservative Middle Eastern and Islamic values, violated in broad daylight by people I should have been able to trust. I was not yet married and had never had this type of contact with any male previously in my life. I didn't know what to do or how to report what had occurred. We were in the middle of the ocean and the Captain of the ship, the most senior authority, was on the flight deck at the time. He must have observed everything that occurred, yet he said nothing.

In relation to Navy's history, this event took place in the early 1990s. It was well before any investigations into abuse associated with events that took place at HMAS *Leeuwin* or the Skype scandal at the Australian Defence Force Academy. It was before the establishment of the Defence Abuse Response Taskforce (DART) which ran between 2012 and 2016 to help people claiming to have suffered physical or sexual abuse, harassment or bullying in the ADF before 2011. It also significantly pre-dated the Me-Too movement that raised awareness and confidence for women to speak up and act against abuse. The safeguards and avenues for appeal back then were not well understood; certainly not by me as a very junior officer unfamiliar with the broad Navy and Defence structure.

Once again, I found myself wondering what good would come of it if I complained. What was done was done. It could never be reversed.

Making My Mark

In the main, my deployment to the USA was highly successful, both personally and professionally. I learned a lot about my role and grew in terms of knowing myself. For me, this growth is a huge part of what a navy career is about. It pushes you on many different fronts. It introduces you to scenarios that challenge and demand, up to - and often beyond - boundaries once thought of as stretched. Through the journey, you often come to realise you can do so much more than you once imagined. You learn and innovate, growing confidence and skills that are invariably passed on to others through example. It is an environment that exposes all aspects of character and provides rich opportunities for leadership at all levels.

My ability to put the initial trauma involving 'King Neptune' behind me, allowed me to appreciate the many other wonderful experiences on offer as I got to know and become friends with most of the crew. Navy deployments are a lot of work but there is plenty of time for relaxation and socialisation.

Our time in Hawaii brought opportunities to go hiking and swimming, followed by relaxing in volcanic-sulphur pools. Hawaii was hot and muggy. This made dips in the ocean incredibly refreshing and provided the perfect environment to support the growth of dense green rainforests, cram-packed with ferns and parasitic vines. This beautiful terrain was only pierced occasionally by the steaming and overly pungent sulphur rock pools. They looked gorgeous and mystical. The tourist brochures presented them as having wonderful therapeutic benefits. Although quite hot and relaxing for the muscles, I was unconvinced that the sulphur was doing me any good. I couldn't stay in that water for long. It remains my view that, when your body is uncontrollably gagging due to a foul smell, this is a good natural indication you probably should remove yourself from the source.

In port, in San Diego, a few of us took leave, rented a Mustang and went on a road trip down to Mexico. Culturally, it was a wonderful experience and very exciting. We had the music on full pelt in the car. We had bought some cassette tapes of American classics and were determined to immerse ourselves in the nation's history, scenic beauty and culture as we sang at the top of our lungs. Tijuana was as far as we got into Mexico. It was a gorgeous town, full of great restaurants and little shops selling all kinds of traditional crafts and memorabilia.

I got right into the action, bargaining hard to secure some treasures to send home as gifts. I had been lured by the wonderful colours and intricate patterns on display in a tiny store that sat on no more than two square metres. The shopkeeper was dressed in a traditional poncho and sombrero, had two missing front teeth and was, surprisingly, shorter than me. I thought I had done really well, knocking off good percentages of the original asking prices. My limited bargaining skills compared to those of the experienced storekeeper only became apparent to me when one of my colleagues pointed out that Mexico didn't have the goods tax I had become accustomed to paying on top of all advertised prices in the US. He certainly got me good! It didn't matter, though, because the experience was way more valuable than any savings I may or may not have made that day.

To top the embarrassment off, I was temporarily detained at the Tijuana border although my colleagues were all ushered through without incident. However, this time, my 'special' treatment could not be put down to being different but, rather, due to my similarities to the Mexicans. My dark skin had authorities suspecting me of being an illegal immigrant who was trying to cross the border. My broad Australian accent and Navy identification card saw me through what could otherwise have been a harrowing occasion.

In Los Angeles, we went to Disneyland. We rode on rollercoasters and enjoyed many movie-themed rides with a scale and ferocity I'd never before encountered in my life. The whole experience was thrilling. Any pent-up stress from the daily routines on the ship was now a distant memory, usurped by the good feelings of childhood fuelled through the consumption of sweet fairy floss and mountains of ice cream.

Then there were the cable cars in San Francisco, elegant in their historic design with timber seats and rails. Some had rope-operated windows and areas where you could sit directly exposed to the elements with no restraints; literally hanging out the side. They provided both a versatile and scenic form of transport across the bay. Most impressively, they clung effortlessly to a complex network of tracks that covered the very steep streets of the city.

I also remember having a great lunch at Fisherman's Wharf. I started with clam chowder, hot and creamy and a must-try in this part of the world. Lobster at the centre of a huge seafood basket topped off what must have been enough food to keep me going for a week.

Refreshed after having spoilt myself silly, I returned with my equally-pampered travel mates to join the ship which had sailed back to Hawaii while we were away.

Of course, the spectre of 'King Neptune' didn't entirely disappear. I hadn't expected him to vanish or for the crew to suddenly change after years of ingrained attitude but there were other 'moments' that tarnished the joy and had me questioning my position here, in this situation, as a woman and as a Muslim.

The luau in Hawaii, for example, was a marvellous event full of bright colour, laughter and joy. It didn't matter that I couldn't eat the meal, which was comprised predominantly of sandpit-baked pork, because I loved the music and the cultural experience that went with it.

Then 'tradition' raised its head.

"It is tradition, here in Hawaii, for a man to kiss a woman as part of the luau proceedings," one of the organisers announced.

Giggles erupted from the rest of the crew but my stomach dropped as I wondered how, as one of the three women present, I would get out of this.

"How about I just give you a quick peck on the cheek?" my boss, who was standing near me, said. "That way, it's not so bad for you but we are still honouring the tradition of our hosts." He smiled and I was pleased he seemed to understand I would not be amenable to any type of passionate encounter.

I nodded, trusting him. However, as he leaned forward for the 'peck', he instead sniffed my cheek weirdly before planting his lips fully and firmly on my face. Why I didn't object straight out at the time, I do not know. Perhaps it was the power imbalance; I felt obliged not to embarrass him and, quite frankly, didn't want the fuss.

However, these moments did not take away from the experience as a whole, because I refused to let them. I couldn't permit the pleasure of special life experiences and events to be stolen from me. That would be nothing more than allowing a denial of my agency.

The entire deployment was like a 'bucket list' tour, with Navy as our host. Everything was perfectly orchestrated, right down to our normal 'wakey wakey', which was broadcast as the ship entered port, being replaced by David Lee Roth's *California Girls*. It was exactly what I'd dreamt of – the adventure, the good times and the great friends.

Life was amazing.

In terms of work, the war games we played with the Americans and other allies went off well. We fired guns and launched missiles and torpedoes. With each evolution, the ship jolted and paint on the superstructure burned. It is incredibly satisfying to hear and feel the loud release of weapons from equipment meticulously maintained on a daily basis and normally quiet. It was evident that all the planning, training and preparation had been effective.

"Fire!" ordered the Gunnery Officer.

I learned at a cracking pace and our task force 'won the war'. However, at the same time, I was also incredibly homesick.

The day of our return came, though, and like the rest of the crew, my key priority became to securely fasten all the large gifts I'd bought for myself and my family in various compartments throughout the ship so they wouldn't be damaged or, more importantly, wouldn't damage any of the equipment. I had bought a petrol-powered bike that was now strapped among the sonar buoys.

Once I'd diligently finished off my journal and task book, there wasn't much left for me to do except to continue to secure VCR cassettes so I could provide the crew with the evening's entertainment. It remained my aim to select a good evening movie the crew could enjoy each night from 8:30 pm, right up to our return to Sydney. I was determined not to disappoint. One night, I found one of the senior officers fumbling around by himself in the isolated compartment where the VCR player was housed. Surprised to see him there, I went in.

"Is something wrong?" I asked. I was sure it hadn't turned 8:30 pm yet.

He looked up and it dawned on me he was there to speak to me privately.

I went straight to the VCR machine and started my normal routine, trying very hard to distract from the awkwardness of the situation. "I hope the crew like this Batman movie tonight," I said, trying to fill the silence. In my mind, I willed him not to say anything.

"Mona," he said softly, his voice uncharacteristically nervous as he talked to my back.

He'd called me Mona. He never called me Mona and certainly never in that tone. It was always a polite and formal Sub-Lieutenant Shindy.

I finished loading the machine and forced my face into a picture of composure before I turned around.

"Yes, Sir?" I said, emphasising the 'Sir'. I had to remind him of the nature of the only relationship we could have.

He got it. "Oh, nothing. Don't worry," he said as he turned and left the compartment.

Nothing more was said.

A few days later, we were home. I got straight into a taxi as soon as leave was piped. Unlike most of the crew, I had no-one on the wharf when the ship docked. It was heartwarming to see all the happy reunions but they made me yearn even more for the love of my own family. With Hassan away, Mum unable to drive and Bida and Freda caught up with studies, I understood why it was difficult for them to be there. Truth is, I had actually told them to stay away, arguing it would be logistically easier for me to come to them only minutes after the ship arrived.

As the taxi pulled up at home, I saw Mum charge through the front door, where she had clearly been waiting in anticipation. I barely finished paying the driver before the car door opened and Mum was halfway in, smothering me with kisses.

"Habebti, I missed you. My baby!" These were the words she used to greet me. It is funny how, in my family at least, a child always remains a baby to someone, no matter how old, independent or accomplished they become.

Mum's smile was warm and her embrace firm and prolonged. I felt instant comfort and a sense that I could completely relax. I was safe. I was unconditionally loved. No-one wanted anything from me and my presence alone was more than enough to satisfy those around me. Mum was at home alone and had clearly been cooking all morning. The aromas of all my favourite foods intertwined with the very familiar scent of Mum's perfume. It didn't matter to her that I'd just eaten breakfast. She expected I would dig right into everything she'd prepared. I did exactly that and was revitalised with every scrumptious mouthful while feeling very blessed to finally be home.

From initially being misguided by my crewmates, they had come around to helping and I'd absorbed enough accurate information to receive an assessment of 'difficult to fault' on my written exams. I completed these exams on the passage home from our deployment. The exams were designed to assess a trainee's depth of understanding of ship procedures and systems and my results indicated my readiness to proceed to an in-person interview assessment.

About a week after the ship's return to Australia, I did my oral board assessment with my boss and two other ship engineers he'd organised from ships berthed alongside ours at Garden Island. In less than an hour, I was qualified. I had my certificate of competency and my 'Officer of the Day' ticket and I was ready to do a future posting as a deputy engineer, looking after a ship on my own and leading a duty watch while it was alongside.

The deployment, with its shared challenges and adventures, had brought the crew together. I felt very much part of the team and well-liked by my colleagues. I had made my mark and was respected as a professional engineer and responsive Divisional Officer. I knew this because other officers were now asking me for advice and sailors in my department were comfortable sharing personal challenges and seeking my assistance to find solutions. My confidence had built during the deployment and I also felt comfortable sharing knowledge and personal feelings with others, which, now more often than not, were reciprocated in kind. Colleagues got to understand the impact they were having on me and others and I suspect appreciated the space I had given many to do that learning, rather than instantly reporting and complaining about previously acceptable cultural practices.

The three females had changed that ship and its culture that year. From deeper conversations to a lifting of standards, we had become much loved. A reminder, I suspect, of the warmth of home.

As the only females sharing very tight living quarters, we got on well together. We would sometimes stay up, talking late into the evening and giving each other advice about events that had occurred or things that were troubling us. We got to learn a lot about each other's hopes and challenges and often shared goodies we had purchased ashore. It was clear to me that we each had formed strong bonds with many of the predominantly-male crew. We could often provide insights to each other as to why certain crew members were behaving a particular way, based on deeper stories they had vulnerably shared with each of us in different scenarios.

Knowing I was a key player in influencing the cultural change that happened on that ship that year gave me an immense sense of pride. At times, it was very hard work, painful and even humiliating, but the improved conditions that emerged for women and men alike were very pleasing rewards.

Chapter 3
Family, Marriage and Children

Number 42

Ever since I'd finished university, Mum had been on a mission to get me married. I liked the idea of finding true love and having a family but I wasn't sure about what seemed to be a very clinical approach Mum had embarked on. Her idea was to ask around for eligible men of an appropriate age who had personality and value traits closely matching my own. One thing my first ship deployment taught me was that taking the time to navigate respectful two-way conversations between different people often uncovers fundamental similarities and leads to growth and improved understanding for all involved. It provides the right environment for trust, common purpose and respect to flourish – key ingredients for any successful collaboration. Mum's approach was straight to the point, with everyone involved understanding 'why they were there' from the very first interaction.

"We need to find you a nice boy," she would say while we lounged around watching Egyptian romance movies during my visits home. Egyptian movies played a big part in my education of the Arabic language and my understanding of my cultural heritage. We all loved watching them together from a very young age. "You can't leave these things too late. How lovely would it be to have a little one running around?"

The practicalities of making things happen, in and around work commitments, were things Mum just took in her stride. In fact, as with most Muslim families, getting single people married is not just the role of the whole family but a community responsibility! With pre-marital relations off the table, marriage is seen as the very favoured vehicle to having a full, happy and well-rounded life.

Mum had a couple of well-connected friends in the Australian Muslim community whom she'd met after Dad died. They saw it as their civic duty to do whatever they could to support the community and a subset of their activities included matchmaking. These wonderful do-gooders would listen out for young peoples' preferences in terms of a potential partner and go about connecting them with suitable matches. I suppose it was a bit like a rudimentary approach to what dating apps seek to do today.

Mum had me 'registered' everywhere!

I don't know what she listed as my preferences, but I am sure 'well educated' and 'good Muslim' would have been her two key criteria. Suffice to say, I was introduced to all kinds of people over an intense three-year period of activity. The period spanned my last year of university, my time at the Naval College and the period I was posted away at sea on my first deployment. These men came in all shapes, heights and colours. They had different cultural heritages. Some were around my age while others were many years older. Some were very handsome and some were not. There were doctors, engineers, scientists and business entrepreneurs. Some had grown up in Australia like me, while others were new arrivals from various corners of the globe. They were all very different to each other but one thing they had in common was that they were professed Muslims.

Some would just arrive at Mum's house with no earlier vetting other than a declaration from the individual that he was Muslim, well-educated, handsome and wonderful. Suffice to say, initial encounters could be extremely awkward. In some cases, I completely refused to meet or even say 'hello' to a few of these visitors. I had a system going with Hassan and Bida whereby they would stand in for me if such a situation arose.

I remember one such time when a man was invited to visit after describing himself over the phone to Mum as "broad, tall and good looking". I don't know why he was invited because that approach would have turned me off instantly! As soon as I saw him exit his vehicle, I ran into my brothers' room, pleading for help. The man was clearly double my age and although tall, as promised, all I could see was the inch-long fingernail on his right pinky.

"Mum!" I protested later. "Stop."

She didn't stop, though, but just got more creative. I'd come home from a period at sea and walk in to find a family had been invited over for dinner. The house would be immaculate with a huge spread of Mum's best cooking on the table. There would be beaming smiles all around and a bright-faced young man to sit either next to or perhaps opposite.

On other occasions, Mum would suggest we attend a community event. "Let's go and chat to these people," she would say, indicating a new group we hadn't seen before. "What a coincidence," she'd then say when we found out there was a son of marrying age.

I loved my mum deeply and would always capitulate and go along with her plotting, just to keep her happy.

From these encounters, I had a number of suitors over a period of time. To be classified as a suitor, they had to fulfil two criteria – they must have indicated an intention to marry me by asking my mother or having their parents ask my mother, and I had to agree I wanted to get to know them better. In other words, they were the 'potentials'.

As a young Muslim woman, getting to know someone better usually involved seeing them again in group settings, meeting up as families or going on a romantic date with my brother in tow as a chaperone. It is strange how many young Muslims live in two different worlds. Normal day-to-day life would involve close interactions with the opposite sex in lecture theatres at university, sitting on public transport or collaborating on projects at work. Then suddenly, there would be some societal and community determination that being seen to be mingling alone with someone would somehow be shameful and potentially affect your reputation and that of your family. Talk about making it hard!

There were a few guys along the way who I saw myself marrying but there was always something, often ridiculously insignificant, that meant one of us decided against a union. On one occasion, I decided I wouldn't progress with a young man because his father had a small disagreement with my mother. On other occasions, the reasons were far more significant.

"Oh no, my wife will not work," one potential said.

"You will, of course, wear a hijab," said another.

Such stipulations were, to me, the first signs of 'control'. It was something I would never allow. I had seen examples of families where very highly educated mothers devoted all their time, effort and energy to the house and children and other examples where friends of mine had agreed to such arrangements. It is not that I don't acknowledge the value in devoting effort to the family, I just believe that everyone needs something more that is done for themselves, and this need not be at the expense of raising good children or supporting a life partner. In fact, when both parties to a marriage are able and encouraged to pursue all their personal and professional passions, they feel more fulfilled. In turn, this often provides a different type of benefit to families in the form of inspiration through example and greater financial freedoms. I could see that some of my friends in this situation were not as happy as they were before marriage when we had shared dreams about future career aspirations and personal interests. I was determined to avoid this situation at all costs.

I was posted to HMAS *Canberra* when I first met Suitor Number 42, so I was going away regularly. We'd seen each other a couple of times when, one night, he said, "I don't think I can do this."

"Do what?" I said.

"Be married to someone who is leaving me all the time."

We went our separate ways. I appreciated his honesty, even though I had hoped he would be able to support me in doing whatever interested me at any point in time. We didn't really know each other well at that stage, and although I understood he wasn't opposed to me having a career, it seemed easy to move on given he was struggling to imagine life with me being away regularly, as I was in my current role.

Over a year later, one of Mum's matchmaking friends mentioned his name.

"Do you remember Mohamed? The man I introduced you to for Mona a while back?"

"Yes, it didn't work out at the time for some reason, even though I'm sure Mona liked him," Mum said.

"Well, his mother called me this morning and said he wants to marry Mona! She wanted me to ask you if she would accept."

I don't know what happened to make him reconsider, though I did wonder if someone in his family had convinced him I could always change my career because nothing is forever. Whatever his reason, I decided to give him and his drop-dead gorgeous green eyes another go.

This time, it was quite different. He came over regularly with different members of his family. He struck me as a relatively shy guy, quite the opposite of his very social and talkative sister.

"Tell Mona about the time we lived in Iraq and what life was like there," she would say, encouraging him to open up to me a little more. "You know, he has been building a house?" A proud older sister, Sana sang his praises every chance she got.

His family were so close to each other and I loved the way he interacted with them all. "Mum, do you need me to pick anything up from the shops on my way home?" he'd ask. "Dad, you don't have to lift that. I'll get it." He was an absolute gentleman and incredibly attentive.

Things moved very quickly. We got engaged and just three months later, at the age of twenty-five, I found myself married to Suitor Number 42. Mohamed.

Married Life

❖

"So, when are you leaving the navy?" he asked.

Mohamed and I had been married less than a week. Throughout our engagement and in the days following our wedding, he'd said nothing. It was framed as an innocent question while we were washing up after dinner.

"What?" I was outraged. I couldn't believe he assumed I would just change my life because I was now married to him. "What do you mean?" And so began our first fight.

For those who are not familiar with married life for Muslims, there are clear structures and expectations as to roles. First and foremost, there is the clear proclamation that 'women are the equal sisters of men'. However, in honour of his wife and the critical role she plays in supporting the family and helping to raise a strong pious community, a husband is obliged to provide fully for her needs and that of their children. She is not required to work or contribute financially and many women within the community choose to do just that. So much so that, sometimes, members in the community might negatively judge a husband who has a wife who works – let alone one who appears to be gallivanting around the world! For some families, the idea of honouring women is sometimes wrongly skewed into a perception of control and restriction. This was certainly not how Mohamed thought, but I know he often encountered commentary from other Muslim men that painted him as weak or disrespected by me in some way.

"Well, don't you think life would be better if we were together all the time?" he said. "There are lots of other jobs you could do that wouldn't take you away."

I raised one eyebrow and placed my hands on my hips, ready to rebut anything he might have to say.

"And we want to start a family straight away, don't we? If you're away – well – it's just not ideal, is it?"

He had a point, in principle, and I knew he was probably right. "You're making assumptions about what I want to do with my life, aren't you?" I argued back. "I've never thought about leaving the navy. It's certainly not something we ever agreed on before getting married."

I was ashore at this time and was enjoying my role, leading a small team running communications equipment trials, tempest testing and radio frequency hazard surveys on our ships. If I'm totally honest, I knew I was probably resisting his suggestions initially, just to make the point that he shouldn't ever think to change me. It was an interesting start to a tumultuous first year together as we adjusted to each other's needs and boundaries and learned to compromise.

Some things were trivial, like the cooking and cleaning, but they were things that we needed to work through just like any other newlyweds. We both came from homes where our mothers did everything for us. I'd assumed we'd share the chores; Mohamed had initially assumed I would do most of it. His nature was to do whatever he could to make me happy and comfortable and he would often go out of his way to help.

"Do you want me to help with chopping up the vegetables?" he would say. Or, "Let me fill up the mop bucket for you."

He would do this kind of thing often and then work his way back to the living room to watch TV or to the bathroom to shower. I trod lightly at first, happy to create nice meals and clean spaces for us to share, all while trying to understand his thought process. Did he think it was my role to do all the household chores? Did he not know what was required or how to go about completing the tasks? As I observed him, it became clear to me that he knew exactly what was required and was also an excellent cook. He demonstrated this through the advice he gave on special ingredients and preparation techniques for meals and his knowledge of cleaning products and applications.

"I'm just as tired as you after work," I pointed out one day when it finally came to a head. I guess he hadn't really thought of it like this before. He seemed startled by my outburst, I'm sure because he thought he was already going above and beyond what was expected of him. He had only ever been familiar with households where women took on all of these roles, generally as their primary and often only activities during the day. I am not sure about the cleaning, but most of the ladies on Mohamed's side absolutely loved cooking and entertaining.

"Right," he said and we sat down and divvied things up. We had moved into a modern, two-bedroom unit in North Sydney, which was within walking distance and just down the road from where I worked. Mohamed travelled across the Harbour Bridge to get to work on the south side of town. The unit had two bathrooms and our ensuite had a spa. We had spent a good part of our three-month engagement buying furniture for our new home. Mohamed was very conscious of his religious requirement to cover all the expenses for the family. I remember him dutifully nodding when we were reminded of this obligation by the Imam at our marriage ceremony. Mohamed looked so cute and serious. He had spent every last cent of his savings buying things that were to my liking. I have never been big on material possessions and would always try to keep my requests practical and reasonably priced. I loved the way he would always alert me to the more expensive and extravagant. We even argued about what he would buy in the way of an engagement and wedding band. I was happy with something small.

"It is enough and safer given that I work around equipment all day. Larger objects are more likely to catch on something," I said. "I have small fingers, too, and these big diamonds look really funny on my hand."

"I want you to have something nice," was his retort. And so our life together went on; Mohamed trying to spend more than necessary, and me dampening his enthusiasm while adopting a more strategic approach to our financial affairs.

I was already covering the rent directly from my pay as it made sense to go through Defence Housing and receive a subsidy as a condition of service. Mohamed paid for everything else.

We shared most duties at home and completed tasks together. We naturally assumed full responsibility for different chores when the other was held back at work or wasn't feeling well. Neither of us needed to ask.

Mohamed adapted to what I needed and wanted – space and support to pursue my career aspirations, contribute financially to the home and be involved in all decision-making that could potentially impact our family unit. For my part, I learned to sacrifice with regard to pursuing career pathways that slowed my progression and had me at home more often. I became better at giving ground to meet Mohamed's needs – wanting to be a father much earlier than I had hoped to be a mother, and spending more time with his large extended family. When I was first introduced to all of them, I remember being quite overwhelmed with all the activity and noise. I'd grown up having never really experienced large family or community gatherings. My family was essentially just Mum and my three siblings.

Mohamed's family would, from time to time, book a community hall for a gathering. Within minutes of arriving, I'd be drawn into their discussions.

"Where did you put the coffee cups?"

"Bilal won't give me a turn holding the ball."

"No! The Liberals won't win the next election."

"Do you want to put in for the building of a well in Afghanistan?"

"I can't make it to the mosque committee meeting at 3 pm. I'm scheduled in to give blood."

"When is the barbecue going to start? I'm starving!"

The daily discussions went on, often one on top of another.

"It's Mahmoud's birthday next week. What do you think he would like as a present?"

"Why are tomatoes so expensive these days?"

"We are going on a family cruise. Do you want to join us?"

"Hanadi punched me!"

"I think Noah is in love with a girl in his class."

"Do you believe the house sold for $1.5 million in Merrylands!"

The constant hum of noise was regularly pierced by the sharp clangs of pots and dishes being washed, whistles from boiling teapots and children screaming and shouting as they played outside. The mayhem was relentless, but always shrouded in love and warmth.

"*Jibili el jisdan.*" Mohamed's mother would ask for something. It took constant inquiry to work out what was going on.

"Jisdan?" I would say.

"It means handbag," Mohamed would advise.

"Oh, we say *shunta* in Egyptian Arabic."

Then there were words such as *soobaat*, which I later understood to be the equivalent of *gasma* in Egyptian. Shoes.

I didn't understand everything that was said to me in the Lebanese dialect of Arabic and struggled to feel comfortable in all their social settings. The learning curve was steep. It is funny how I now consider these things among the most precious joys in my life. I feel so blessed that he was able to talk me into everything he did.

Later, once our children were born, I learned how to sacrifice all over again – just like any other parent. None of us are superhuman. The success of our marriage relied on us sharing everything and playing to our individual strengths. For me, this meant helping with the kids' homework and handling all the paperwork and financial administration. For Mohamed, it was all the labouring and handyman jobs around the house, including doing most of the laundry. We played tag team with the kids a lot but managed to work out routines that meant we had many wonderful times together as a complete unit, while still meeting all their needs as single carers.

To be fair, though, although we agreed on sharing equally, Mohamed has always willingly tackled a lot of the day-to-day household work. He's all about making sure his family is well taken care of and happy. He will never leave the house without asking if I need something from outside and always buys things just because he knows someone at home likes them. No special occasions are required. I love this about him and I know how lucky I am.

After our initial disagreement all those years ago, I ended up staying with Navy for thirty-two years and was supported and encouraged by Mohamed every step of the way. He put up with a lot. He tolerated my absences from home, put his career on hold, managed the house and kids as a 'solo parent' while I was away and even had his manhood questioned by many community members, time and time again.

Shattering Identity Bias

"Why are you doing everything? How can you tolerate her going away for so long? She should be at home looking after you and the kids!"

"I'd trade her in for another if I was you! Why don't you just tell her to stay home? What's wrong with you?"

"It is her career," Mohamed would reply. "She has worked really hard to get to where she is. I'm going to support her. Just mind your own business h*abiby!*" Mohamed would reply to his mates.

Mohamed is my rock and, second only to my mum, my loudest cheerleader. For this, I am extremely grateful.

Mona Shindy

Chapter 4
Organisational Leadership, War and Success

Gaining Respect

Through the love and support of my family, I not only met all my Navy appointments and obligations but excelled in them.

Early on in my career, it was quite uncommon for 'mothers' to go to sea. Indeed, not too many years earlier, marriage meant a woman's career would be over. I can't say I was delighted about leaving my young children, but if I had any hope of progressing and moving up the ranks, I had to finalise several, now mandatory, sea obligations.

At the time, the newly adopted policy had become: You shouldn't be in uniform if you are not going to sea. It was Navy's first attempt to fully integrate women into all roles and disciplines.

For the first time in my career, I felt my employer had breached my psychological contract with the organisation. The recruiters had been very clear about my options to choose if or when I might like to take a position on a ship.

"There are so many career paths you could follow in the navy. As an engineer, the opportunities are rich and varied. You can chop and change too," the female Lieutenant said at the recruitment office.

"So, there is flexibility and opportunities to move around and work with different technologies? Opportunities to travel abroad?" I asked. "What about having a family in the future and spending more time grounded?"

I wanted to understand my options and imagine what my life might look like if my personal circumstances changed.

"Yes, of course. All of that is possible. In fact, you don't have to go to sea at all if you don't want to. There is a stream called 'shore communications' that I'm sure your electrical engineering qualifications would be ideal for."

In truth, though, what the recruiters had sold was not practical when it came to manpower allocation, career advancement training and development, and the creation of sustainable sea-shore rotation rosters. Firstly, there wasn't enough personnel. Secondly, training and upskilling processes were already complex and costly. These two factors created the need for standardised career progression pathways, against which we had to adapt our lives to meet. Not the other way round.

I remember asking a question of the Fleet Weapons Electrical Engineer during an engineer's information session for the introduction of these new pathways.

"But, Sir," I said when he'd paused for questions. We were in a large auditorium filled with about one hundred engineers who had come together from the various bases and ships alongside in Sydney at the time. I was one of five females listening intently in the audience. "When is a woman meant to have children in that sequence of events and postings?" I knew I'd be challenging my biological clock by the end of my pathway.

"Well, that is not my problem. You will just have to work it out."

It was a harsh response but typical for the day. I slumped back into my chair, despondent. Devalued and unappreciated were two words that sprang to mind. Plus, I was actually quite disgusted by the arrogance in his tone. It was a style he had clearly become accustomed to, staring me directly in the eyes, knowing with absolute certainty that our difference in rank would mitigate any risk of me having any further comeback. I fell silent, my attention taken by the sick feeling I now had in my stomach.

Then the laughter started from what seemed like every corner of the auditorium – also typical for that era in a male-dominated environment. The sort of laughter designed to agree with and suck up to a senior officer for his 'witty' response.

To me, though, the response I received to a legitimate question just seemed poor and not well considered. As with many things in the navy, the new career pathways would be implemented as soon as they were signed off by the head of the community. The options were to either fall into line, resign or stagnate at the same rank until it was determined that your retention would no longer be in the interest of the navy.

Something changes in you when you become a mother. I struggled with leaving my babies at childcare – how could I possibly be away from them for months on end?

The navy was also struggling with how to communicate with its female personnel. There were sensitivities around asking women what their plans were for family and many discussions took place concerning what was and wasn't permissible under the Anti-Discrimination Act.

At one point, I was asked to write a letter explaining my future plans for child-bearing and when I would be available to take up my next sea appointment. I was sure the hierarchy had written me off as unlikely to ever go back to sea; I was a woman from a conservative, Middle Eastern, Islamic background – what were the chances?

Many women did their talking with their feet and left the service. They had assessed that what was being asked of them was incompatible with family obligations and their desire to have and nurture children. That was their choice – albeit a forced one.

Up until this point, I had resisted going to sea and leaving behind my two young children, both in their formative years. Being forced to choose and then justify my choices through a letter did not sit well with me or my identity as a mother and as an employee of the navy.

I loved my kids but I also loved my navy career and my colleagues and thoroughly enjoyed every job and every piece of cutting-edge technology I was exposed to. "If the navy can wait until the kids are in a more structured schooling arrangement, then you and Mum could combine forces to take care of them while I'm away. What do you think?" I said when I finally broached the topic with Mum and Mohamed.

Mum was all in. Her mission in life was to see her kids fly. She would do almost anything. My new proposal now involved more time with the adorable grandkids, so she encouraged me to go for it.

Mohamed, however, was not hugely excited about the idea. "I want you to be happy," he responded, but I could see he needed more assurance.

Over several weeks and many deep conversations with Mohamed, I drew out likely career trajectories, mapped out ship maintenance periods when I would be alongside in Sydney and argued my absences to be short-term sacrifices against the potential for a much longer and incredibly rewarding professional career. "I've worked so hard to get to this stage in my career," I said. "I don't want to throw it away for something I know we are strong enough to overcome as a family."

Eventually, we made the commitment. Psychologically and practically, we prepared for what was ahead.

After careful consideration and consultation with family, I am able to advise that I will be ready to take up a sea posting six months from today to align with position rotation timings in the new year. As my husband will be taking leave from work to act as the primary caregiver for our children, I am seeking concurrence and support to complete back-to-back sea postings as a deputy engineer, then as the head of the department directly afterwards. This would be the most manageable sequence of events for us as a family.

I wrote this as clearly as I could – formal and precise so there was no misunderstanding.

I showed Mohamed how to access our financial accounts online and pay bills. I wrote him notes on what to do if certain events occurred and how to contact Defence Support Organisations. We worked through potential scenarios with me quizzing him on his proposed course of action. Over time, his confidence built and my worries reduced.

We reassured ourselves. "We've got this!"

Six months after I'd started this conversation with Mohamed, I was posted to HMAS *Sydney* as Deputy Weapons Electrical Engineer. It was a two-year appointment, after which I would take a short-term shore job before returning to sea for one final two-year appointment as the head of the Weapons Electrical Engineering Department. Combined, this would finalise my sea obligations. In the process, I would be promoted up two ranks and be set to tackle many other technically challenging roles I aspired to perform. I knew I could do it!

As with any well laid out plan, there were many times we needed to adjust as a family. Mum's enthusiasm was soon dampened by the realities of caring for demanding youngsters who were always on the go. The addition of Hassan's kids to 'Grandma's home childcare' became too much in the end, but I am very much indebted to Mum for how she always supported me in life. Her limitless belief in me would often lead to her own overload as she pushed me forward with every ounce of her being. I will forever love her.

With me having made the commitment in writing to return to sea, Mohamed felt obliged to take on the role of full-time carer for the children when Mum could no longer help. He took all his leave and then some extra time without pay to cover the periods I was away.

It wasn't only the challenges of raising the kids and managing the house that Mohamed had to contend with on his own. He was also fending off criticism from some community members, all while still seeking, wanting and needing to engage with them for love and support. We both walked tightropes and made many sacrifices to make things work.

I hated missing important milestones, like birthdays and Eid at the end of Ramadan. Fasting alone amidst a non-Muslim crew was certainly more difficult than having the excitement and abundance of family gatherings. The dinner meal portion sizes at sea, although hearty, were not enough to compensate for a normal calorie intake over three meals. I sometimes slept hungry or topped up with unhealthy snacks sourced from the ship's canteen. The stewards and cooks took rationing seriously to make sure supplies lasted. They didn't quite appreciate what fasting actually meant for me. I sometimes felt quite isolated and lonely.

Interestingly, my son recently told me that on his ship, the stewards always asked if he needed extras while fasting.

"Do you want us to put an extra plate aside for you in the pantry just in case you get hungry again later in the evening?" they would say.

I like to think there has been a gradual increase in awareness and sensitivity; some of it in part due to the contributions and sacrifices of culturally diverse people while serving over the years.

Without a doubt, however, the thing that most troubled me while I was away was the constant worry about Mohamed and the kids. I stressed about whether they had enough emotional support. I felt guilty about abandoning them. I constantly worried that my children would be irreversibly damaged. I felt selfish. In many ways, I constantly grieved for the myriad of very normal experiences most families enjoyed and struggled with together through the mundane routines of life.

Although Mohamed's face in old home videos does not always say it, this experience was great for us as a family. He is incredibly close to our kids; a relationship not all dads get the opportunity to develop.

Mona Shindy

Being Away

On returning to sea, I was immediately off on a North Asian deployment – this time with a lot more responsibility. As the Deputy Weapons Electrical Engineer on the ship, I was responsible for all aspects of how my department ran. From overseeing and leading the alignment and maintenance of the weapons systems and the ship's explosive ordnance, to ensuring the welfare of the sailors in my charge, my duties were many and varied. I was also required to develop and support the trainee engineers.

It had been eight years since I served on a ship and twelve years since I had left the Australian station on deployment. Things had changed significantly in that time. Women represented a good twenty per cent of the ship's company. There was no longer any smoking within the ship's superstructure and drinking was prohibited during lunchtime working hours.

The atmosphere in the wardroom had also changed. With a higher percentage of women, I noticed all spaces within the ship were more inviting, with a more civil atmosphere. This was particularly evident in the accommodation and recreation areas, where it was now understood that posters of naked women, pornographic videos and unrestrained swearing were not acceptable.

Conversations and discussions between crew members were less superficial and now incorporated acknowledgments of feelings and hopes. My team regularly talked to me about their dreams and disappointments, and sought advice and support on a more emotional level. This concept would have been totally out of the question for the one hundred per cent male crew of the past, where any such display of emotions would be ridiculed as a sign of weakness. A friendly, working relationship with male colleagues was now easier to have as their wives had accepted that women at sea were there in a professional capacity and not necessarily looking to steal their partners away.

Despite these improvements, it was hard being away from family and the situation was worsened by the relationship I had with my boss. He came across to me as being somewhat introverted and apart from being highly judgemental about how I completed my duties, he adopted the approach of full delegation. I felt I was doing most of his job as well as my own.

At first, it was the little putdowns. "Don't you know how many sonar buoys we have on board? You should be keeping track of those."

Then came the overloading of assigned tasks, many of which were ones he was supposed to carry out. I would be given special sea dutyman's responsibilities on the bridge if we were entering a constricted port in the early hours of the morning, or asked to resolve welfare matters for his direct reports. The section heads were instructed to tell him immediately if there were any faults in the systems. "Shindy," he would say after calling me to his cabin upon receiving any such reports, "why were you unaware of the oil leak on the missile launcher?"

These extra responsibilities, and constantly being on edge waiting for the next judgement, meant I had very little time during the day or evening for my personal activities or just to relax.

He was a single man with no children or life partner at the time. I suspect he may possibly have been a little envious of my family situation but this didn't necessitate what I perceived to be abuse of power, nor should it have led to him making my life miserable at every opportunity.

I loved talking about my husband and kids and was always planning for my next rendezvous with them. I tried to take some leave mid-deployment to fly home and break up the time away while the ship was on passage. I'd worked very hard to clear all the tasks on my plate. I even proposed doing most of the ship caretaker duties while the ship was in foreign ports so others could get away and enjoy their time in the different locations we would visit.

"No," he argued. "Absolutely not. The ship needs the Deputy Weapons Electrical Engineer at all times."

It was true there could be equipment failures at any time and that the department had established processes where my position was central to its efficient operations. His position, therefore, on what was required of me had merit, based on established and existing practices. I could understand and accept that, but the complete unwillingness to explore or entertain alternate approaches or suggestions was frustrating.

At the time, because of the strange looks given me, I also suspected my boss was envious of the relationships I had with the subordinates within the department. I was the one who was present with them at all times while he stayed in his cabin for much of the day. He also ate on his own during evening steel-deck barbecues and I could feel his glare as I sat, chatting with the group. I wasn't sure how he expected to build relationships.

Nevertheless, I worked around the 'roadblocks' I felt were put in place – the initiatives to assert dominance over me through putdowns and his constant agenda to demonstrate how much more he knew than I did. He did know a lot and I respected that. He was well-read and had clearly spent many hours understanding the ship's systems inside out. It's exactly what I expected from the head of the Weapons Electrical Engineering Department.

What surprised me was what felt like an aversion to teamwork and mentoring – crucial responsibilities to achieve an efficient, collegiate and effective organisation. After all, I was there as the deputy to continue building my skill sets and be assessed as competent to lead the department at the end of my two-year posting.

Mona Shindy

If there is one thing I am really good at, it is finding ways to make things work. Resilience, innovation and adaptability are core character traits of mine. Upon realising he had directed immediate information flow to him, I set about leveraging my strong relationships to ensure I was never again compromised. The team didn't find it at all inconvenient to brief me on issues before they – and more often than not, I – directly briefed the boss on the ship's state of affairs. I distracted myself from the intense homesickness through regular exercise and immersing myself in professional development.

Keeping in touch, contributing to the education of my kids and 'being home' in some form, despite my physical absence, required some creativity. I mastered the art of creating care packages that I would mail home from every port. Each care package had a video of me talking about what I had been up to and the places I'd visited. I'd enclose exotic presents along with lots of mundane activities to simulate being at home with the family. I'd record myself reading picture books for Mohamed to play to the kids before they went to bed. I enclosed empty chocolate bar wrappers and asked the kids to dispose of them in the garbage bin.

Of course, this triggered the kids' fascination and their desire to be just as creative. They reciprocated with their own creative care packages that I eagerly awaited as the ship pulled into various ports during the longer deployments. When I opened these packages, there they would be – my little babies telling me about what they learned at school or what mischief the neighbours' kids – never them, of course – had been up to.

"Mum, we won the soccer competition! We are the regional champions," my son would advise.

"Julie had a fight with Rebecca down the street. She called her a rude word!" my daughter would follow.

Their care packages were full of unopened chocolate bars. I shared these with everyone on board the ship, particularly those who didn't have much contact with home. I lived for those parcels. They were vital for my peace of mind. They reduced my worry and calmed my heart. It was not long before my little video camera and tripod were also being shared with other members of the ships' company who wanted to connect more with their families.

Mohamed emailed daily. His emails were the first thing I looked at as soon as I woke up. For a person not big on writing, Mohamed's emails were great. Short and very standard in format, he would tell me everything was okay and the kids were well before going on to describe what he had cooked for dinner the previous night. These emails painted a calm, effectively functioning and controlled environment in which the kids were flourishing. It wasn't until I arrived home that I heard about the car accidents, financial dramas or any near-death experiences the kids had falling from play equipment. By then it was too late to get stressed as those situations had inevitably been overtaken by subsequent events.

As a family, we had learned a system to survive.

We were lucky. At that time, the navy was still losing a lot of well-trained staff, with many people–mothers in particular–finding it hard to remain away at sea for long periods. Societal norms were also changing and fathers were assuming greater responsibility for child-rearing.

Connectivity with home had increased via email and various internet applications. These advancements in communication and expectations were blessings for those deployed, but also created new challenges by blurring what had been a firm and opaque divide between work and home. Tried and proven formulas are great when the environment they are applied to is unchanged. However, they are also often the root cause of decline and failure when rigidly enforced as the world changes.

The navy has adapted brilliantly over the years with those who followed me benefitting from many initiatives born from the struggles my generation endured. It is now common practice for members to be given the opportunity to fly home early at the end of operational deployments before the ship sails back via a longer voyage.

Family support services have advanced considerably and there is a genuine focus on trying to engineer career paths to meet the needs of families, without compromising operational and mission objectives. It is still hard, but knowing that a will exists to think outside the box, and to be creative and flexible where possible, is all that is needed to maintain a strong and committed relationship between Navy and those that serve.

As is the nature of life in the military, the world's uncertainty can have a dramatic impact on government expectations of the armed forces at any given moment in time. Indeed, many of the daily activities at sea are comprised of training scenarios simulating warlike events. Being ready to defend the nation and its interests is the fundamental concern of militaries in peacetime so when called upon, they will be ready to meet government objectives during times of conflict.

Achieving these goals does not come without sacrifice. It was something I'd been willing to do, but I'd be lying if I said it wasn't hard.

My return home from the North Asian deployment was amazing. Separation and arduous conditions are highly effective in crystallising the value of family and home in the minds of the most non-reflective and non-appreciative among us. Embracing a loved one after a long absence is like being enveloped in a soft, warm blanket on a freezing night.

The quiet of the first night at home, away from the constant machinery hum from within the hard and cold shipboard, factory-type environment is bliss. The freedom to move at will outside confined spaces and the vibrant and sumptuous fresh spices in food are unforgettable sensations, etched forever in memory. These experiences would always contribute to the immense gratitude that I would revel in for many days after my return home. Still to this day, these memories sit at the forefront of my mind as I reflect on that period of my life.

Mona Shindy

War

The 2003 Gulf War commenced with a 'shock and awe campaign' spearheaded by the Americans. Honouring its long alliance history with the USA, Australia was one of the 'nations of the willing' ready to address a perceived international threat presented by Saddam Hussein in Iraq through the manufacture and potential use of weapons of mass destruction. As the bombardment of Baghdad commenced, my ship, HMAS Sydney, was steaming at speed to join the Americans and other coalition forces in the Middle East.

Our movement and deployment to war happened within days of the government's announcement. It would have appeared to any onlooker that we had mobilised and responded like a well-oiled machine, sworn and obliged as an instrument of government to act on orders. This is exactly what I signed up for and it is exactly what I did, notwithstanding the unease that engulfed me and many in my family and extended friendship group.

"How do you reconcile your moral values with the possibility of being expected to act in wars that might not be justified and that might result in death and destruction for many innocent people?" It was a question I was asked often.

To be honest, it was and still is difficult to answer, particularly when decisions made by elected governments are not always clear-cut or made along the same set of values or priorities we choose to live by. Being a Muslim in Australia at that time was already extremely challenging. The community was particularly marginalised and subjected to a fair bit of resentment and hostility after the horrific events of 9/11 in New York some two years earlier. There was concern that political decisions being made might be more about punishing the entire Muslim faith group rather than addressing a genuinely confirmed threat. Academic papers and books written by researchers such as Randa Abdel-Fattah, Shakira Hussein and Yassir Morsi go a long way to describing Australian Muslim experiences as those of suspects, not to be trusted in an overarching climate of fear under the idea of a 'war on terror'. For me, the challenges I faced in both a personal and professional capacity felt very similar, with my life choices placing me at odds with the common opinions and views held by many players within the various communities to which I belonged.

However, the role of the profession of arms is not to question decisions made by the democratically-elected government of the day. It must be prepared to act without debate on the direction of a government entrusted by the people of a nation to protect those who elected it. The forums for debate and disagreement are elsewhere and the consequences for the government are determined by the people through electoral processes. At the time, there was much debate within Australian society about the reasonableness of the action against Iraq and the lack of evidence regarding weapons of mass destruction apparently presenting an imminent threat to the world. There certainly was no broad consensus that we should be at war.

International inspectors had not found evidence of dangerous stockpiles of weapons of mass destruction although evidence existed that groups within Iraq had suffered deaths attributable to chemical or biological agents. Many of our preparations leading to the Middle Eastern deployment focused on protecting ourselves from such weapons. We learned to effectively and quickly don gas masks and were expected to take a series of anthrax injections before the ship sailed off to war.

The international community had not determined the legitimacy of a case for war via the passing of any United Nations resolution and there was great uncertainty about the accuracy of claims being made by politicians in the West.

The whole situation completely freaked my mother out. "We have seen nothing to justify us attacking Iraq! These politicians seem to fabricate stories to try and justify war. Just because Saddam refuses to be a puppet for the West. Why are we focused on him? There are lots of bad things happening in many corners of the world. They just want to ruin the country and have the people suffer. To keep them down."

Her unease came off the back of enduring years of discrimination and suspicion of Muslims in Australia. She had watched her son be ridiculed out of Navy, made fun of by colleagues and accused of having the potential to be disloyal or somehow aligned to terrorist movements or agendas. She herself had been spat at on the streets and cursed at for no other reason than she wore a hijab. To put it lightly, her level of trust in the motivations of the Australian government was shaken. After all, that very government should have been protecting and governing for all Australians, not contributing to discussions and rhetoric that isolated and marginalised a section of Australian society – those who were adherents to Islam or those with Arab lineage.

Her unease with the behaviour of government and sections of the media, who appeared to purposely amplify the marginalisation, was something she had grown to live with. She could rationalise how political objectives fuelled the hatred and she gained strength standing in solidarity with fellow Australians who were also adversely affected. She trusted in the intrinsic good of humanity and was hopeful that, in time, such behaviours would not be supported by an intelligent voting public eager for a different type of leadership and a positive national vibe.

What made things almost intolerable for Mum, however, was that the evidence of imminent threat was lacking and I was now being expected to take anthrax inoculations before I could deploy.

"I don't want you taking that poison, Mona. It is not proven to be safe," Mum said in what appeared to be an absolute panic.

Always protective, the idea I would be injected with what was then not a proven or widely used agent was enough for her to insist I refuse the injections and not deploy. I also suspect she understood it would be a convenient excuse to keep me away from a war that had not been adequately justified by the government of the day.

I had read extensively about the vaccine and was satisfied that the known relevant risks were minimal, especially as I was not planning to have any more children. Like my mother and many other Australians at the time, however, I also had significant doubts about the legitimacy of the case for war.

I remember having a heartfelt discussion with the ship's executive officer in the days leading up to the deployment. On a clear night, in the lead-up to our deployment, I stood on the flight deck with my executive officer, overseeing the loading of the last deployment deliveries.

"Are you scared?" he asked.

"I am," I said. "But more about the possibility of killing innocent people."

He nodded.

"I want to go to my grave with a clear conscience and to stand before God, able to justify all my worldly actions and decisions," I said.

He looked at me and, somehow, I just knew he understood and shared the same human values.

"Some of the things people are saying, here on the ship, are disgusting. They're unsettling," I added. "Why is there such excitement around the receipt of extra allowances or the award of a medal? They're so trivial against the inevitable consequences of war."

I was really troubled by how certain members of my ship's company appeared to be singularly focused on personal gain. In recognition of the risks people face when they enter harm's way, extra allowances are paid for the duration of time they remain in a war zone and medals are issued to recognise the sacrifices made in the service of country.

"It will be alright," he assured me. "The real aggression will be left to the Americans. As Australians, our contribution is more aimed at securing Australia's long-term security interests, should we ever be threatened. It will allow us to call for assistance from our much stronger American allies." He paused. "And we'll be positioned well back from any offensive military action."

It was one of the very few times in my life that I disregarded my mother's wishes and stayed the course alongside my shipmates who I had trained with and led. It was not the time to be projecting indecision or jumping ship. For me, I felt a strong obligation to set the right example, remain strong and reassure my team that we would be okay. We would exercise all our jointly-developed skills and capitalise on our extensive training to complete the mission at hand and return home safely. From a mission perspective, I was also confident that our rules of engagement and our secondary alliance role would distance us from actions that could potentially lead to the loss of innocent lives.

The ship was a hive of activity. There were many last-minute equipment additions, ballistic protection, stores and food top-ups before we sailed. Deep discussions, similar to the one I had with the executive officer, also permeated among some of the senior sailors, in the officers' wardroom and in many compartments throughout the ship.

Many in the crew had disclosed concerns about the government's decision for war against the backdrop of what appeared then, and what has been confirmed since, to be unsubstantiated claims of the existence of weapons of mass destruction.

At one point, I also confided in my very close colleagues that members of my extended family – most vocally, my mother – had expressed a desire for me not to go. Unsurprisingly, it was not long before I was called to my boss' cabin for what felt like a very inappropriate interrogation regarding my loyalty and commitment based on my religious affiliation.

"I heard you are a Muslim. Is that going to be a problem?" he asked in a most suspicious tone, alienating me instantly. I couldn't believe it. The years of my contribution to the ADF and my sacrifices were instantly undone because I was now being viewed as suspicious; like I was somehow inherently radical or untrustworthy. I felt helpless, affected by things outside my control where my identity was being defined by others.

"No, Sir. My religion is not a problem." What else could I say or do? Why on earth would I ever wish to harm my friends and colleagues who were, like me, upright citizens just trying to do the right thing by their families and the nation?

It seemed that, unlike any other crew member, I could not express a view about prevailing facts without my religion being used to make me feel like a disloyal outsider and threat to the team. What was clear to me was that the rampant negative public discourse about Muslims had managed to rattle many of my colleagues, creating a perception that I was potentially a danger to them. It is hard enough leaving a husband and young children to go to war but absolutely devastating to have your second family at sea questioning your allegiance. This reality, more than any fear of death in action or side effects from inoculations, was the thing that most made me question whether or not I should continue my career serving my nation.

Dismissed from my boss' cabin, I took myself back to the central office compartment and got on with the job of readying myself and my team for the mission ahead.

Shattering Identity Bias

The passage over to the Middle East Area of Operations was characterised by intense training serials. We simulated coming under attack and the ship taking damage. With each evolution, we refined our skills and readiness to respond. It was not long before we could totally close up the ship and have every member of the crew manning their allocated station ready for action in under two minutes. It was a serious situation that we had embarked on and absolutely everyone was focused on being the best they could be for the team. To think we could have people wake from sleep or step out of the shower and be fully dressed in combat attire ready to fight at their designated action station, which might be at one extreme end of the ship, in under two minutes is amazing.

It was something completely new for most people on the ship, many of whom, like myself, had never been sent to war before and were apprehensive – worried we might never come home to our families again. It is a situation in which the compartmentalising of thoughts is necessary to survive and effectively perform. I immersed myself in my work and developed a routine that limited opportunities for me to dwell on the possibility of tragedy. From working with the sailors to test weapons systems in the dark of night, ensuring the satisfactory completion of all preventative and corrective maintenance, to providing professional and emotional support to all in my charge, I had very little time to worry about much else. We grew as a team and became tighter than ever as a group of people completely reliant on each other to perform and survive.

Or so I thought.

I was engaged in pistol training out on the flight deck. The ship's Bosun's Mates had set up some paper targets at the rear of the vessel. Everything was going very smoothly until it was my turn to step up and shoot. I have always struggled to easily apply sufficient force to the trigger of a 9 mm pistol to get the weapon to fire. My hand and fingers have never been quite strong or long enough to facilitate a comfortable grip. After not effectively discharging my weapon on the order to fire,

I remember turning my head around to explain the situation to the instructors. Clearly unsure of my potential actions, members of the crew scurried for cover, diving for safety behind equipment stored in the ship's hangers.

So it was then, in a brief few moments on one beautifully sunny afternoon as we crossed the equator, my unwavering unity with the team was, again, shaken. The image is something I still live with and, I suspect, will hurt me forever.

This had started to become a recurring theme in my career. I had always worked hard to be accepted, to excel at duties and to develop and protect those around me to build trust and rapport. Somehow, however, no matter what I did, it was apparent my colleagues found it difficult to truly trust me. It seemed like nothing was ever enough to achieve and feel true belonging; either in my mind or in the minds of my colleagues. It meant that I needed to work many times harder than others to prove my worth but I was also likely to be overlooked for opportunities due to some perceived risk associated with my differences from the majority. Not only was my physical appearance different to most but my cultural and religious background was too. All characteristics, I regularly displayed, that others feared.
Yet, I endured.

Even though I didn't like it at all, I would always rationalise these behaviours and forgive those who marginalised me. We lived in an era of constant media and political narrative that presented Muslims as evil, dangerous and intolerant of others. People were fed regular information that taught them to be suspicious and scared of me.

We lived in very close quarters on the ship and inevitably some would get to know me very well. I knew I was truly accepted and respected when I would hear statements like, "But you're not really a practising Muslim!" How ironic. I was truly a very practising Muslim.

Conversely, there were the assessments made of me by some in the Australian Muslim community. "You can't be a true Muslim, going off to kill innocent people and damage an ancient society in an unjustified war."

I have always made the effort to understand and explore the reasoning, values and drivers in the various environments I see myself as belonging, in order to find a comfortable position to sit. For me, that position has always been in the common area of intersecting circles that each define the collective values of the often-segregated communities. What I have learned is that although I am comfortable drawing boundaries in relation to what I will take from each community, many struggle to see all scenarios as anything other than black or white. They define belonging as an 'all or nothing' concept. For me, what is reasonable or true often lies in the grey, requiring nuance to discover.

The deployment continued for several months, interspersed with opportunities for some rest and respite in a few Middle Eastern ports. When we got to Dubai, the ship's company were permitted to rent rooms in some predetermined city hotels. I chose to stay on the ship and spend my money on presents for the kids. "What do you know that we don't?" a colleague asked me. He turned to the other officers in the wardroom and said, "We should just do what Mona is doing because she would know if the hotels are likely to be attacked by terrorists."

Once again, a sickly giggle rippled through the mess. It was as though they thought I wouldn't find the comment offensive and completely inappropriate. In that moment, as was common practice for me in these scenarios, I shut down, maintained a blank expression and said nothing. It was, I suppose, more of a survival mechanism . The era was one where, as a Muslim, I constantly felt as though I was stuck in a binary. Was I seen as 'good' and deserving of inclusion, friendship and trust? Or was I 'bad' and a radical threat to be guarded against?

The main war was virtually over before we arrived on station and we spent most of our time patrolling to disrupt pirates and the illegal trade now rampant due to the dismantling of law enforcement and structured government control in the region. Besides questioning my loyalty every so often, many in the crew were also happy and eager to tag along shopping with me whenever they could. It is funny how people always feel more comfortable with those they can relate to easily. My rudimentary Arabic skills always meant I could get better deals from shopkeepers on their behalf! That is something I was easily trusted with.

We finished our rotation in the Middle East without serious incident. There were some close and uneasy interactions with Iranian naval vessels and scuffles on ships our teams boarded when illegal cargo was discovered but, overall, it was an incredibly successful mission. We had done what was expected of us and we were on our way home.

By this time in the navy's history, there was more flexibility with how we managed the manning of ships while deployed. There was an opportunity for some members of the crew to fly back to Australia early as the ship weaved its way home via some respite ports. The idea was that those who went home early would look after the ship when it returned as the remaining crew had a good window to spend with family before resuming duties. I was missing my family immensely by this stage and was among the volunteers to head home early. I willingly missed India's adventures and gastronomic excitement to embrace Mohamed and the kids instead, at the first possible opportunity.

It was worth it. True heaven. Everyone was delighted to see me. Extended family came from everywhere. Mohamed had cooked all my favourite foods. The kids seemed so much bigger. It is hard to find the words to describe how happy I was.

So much happened in that first twenty-four hours home, including getting pregnant with my youngest child!

I was furious. We had made so many sacrifices as a family. We had an agreement. How was I going to go back to sea to finish my final two-year sea obligation as the head of the Weapons Electrical Engineering Department? I couldn't be on a ship while pregnant. This would derail the plan I had agreed to with the Navy; it would halt the career progression trajectory I had negotiated and would negate the significant separation sacrifice we had just made.

My intense anger soon turned to trepidation when I remembered all the fuss people had been making about the unknown impacts on the foetus in mothers who had received anthrax injections. Things changed quickly and I needed time to process the new uncertainties. I was shocked, scared and angry all at once. At the same time, I was secretly delighted at the thought of being a new mother once again.

Mona Shindy

Building and Supporting Navy Growth

Some months later, I honoured the plan I had with Navy and joined HMAS *Melbourne* as the Weapons Electrical Engineering Head of Department.

Having walked across the gangway in casual attire, I was greeted by an overzealous Quartermaster who was determined to exercise authority over me. It was not until I flashed my identification card and introduced myself as the ship's new Weapons Electrical Engineering Officer (WEEO) that I saw any form of respect.

"Oh ... hello, Ma'am. Welcome aboard."

"Is that the WEEO?" the assistant Quartermaster whispered with more than a tinge of disbelief in her voice as I strolled down the breezeway towards the Captain's cabin. Things were slowly changing, with a female manning the gangway, but still not to the point that someone who looked like me would automatically be assumed to hold any important or influential position.

My career managers had tried to do the right thing to support me and my family when I was posted to HMAS *Melbourne*. The ship was one of Navy's Adelaide Class frigates that were sequentially being put through an upgrade program at the time. This meant each ship would spend six months in deep maintenance while it was refurbished with a range of new equipment and technologies. Crew members could do an honest day's work and still go home to their families each night.

Originally, before anyone knew I was pregnant, I had been allocated to one of the frigates due to be out of the program and engaged in missions, potentially anywhere around the world. To my surprise, while I was on maternity leave, the powers from above, decided to change my posting to HMAS *Melbourne* as she was scheduled to be entering the upgrade program as I returned from leave. Someone was actively mitigating risks both to families and ships' programs by considering any compelling personal circumstances before trying to match individuals to the most appropriate vessels.

"You're kidding?" I said out loud as I read the email with my posting orders attached. I looked at Mohamed. "You'd think they could've run it by me first."

I'd already psyched myself up and prepared mentally for potential deployment. Although I understood the rationale and could accept why the change was made, I still felt managed and untrusted to deliver.

As with any well-laid plans, however, nothing is guaranteed. Due to delays with the first ship in upgrade, HMAS *Melbourne* would be engaged in a range of deployments that would have her away from the Australian station for long periods – commencing as soon as I joined her.

Mohamed was devastated. "Wasn't this new ship meant to be alongside in maintenance for a while? Are you really leaving straight away?" he asked, clearly dealing with a roller-coaster of emotions and worrying about how he would cope solo. Our family was like an island in many ways, with no real tangible or practical support available to us through work. We had help in the form of 'talking to someone' but no-one was coming over to assist with childcare or the laundry.

Our baby was only five months old when I joined that ship and I was still breastfeeding the morning we sailed for a three-month mission. I'd left a couple of bottles of breast milk in the fridge and had been introducing powdered milk to the baby in the preceding month but she didn't really like it. I will never forget the look on Mohamed's face as I said goodbye to him and the kids. He was scared.

I cannot adequately describe how I felt as I left the house that morning. I left them all in my bed, turned and went down the stairs, not daring to look back. I was abandoning my family at a time they desperately needed me. To say I felt dreadful is an understatement; it was like a knife in the heart. Here I was, allowing my family to suffer so I could meet a career milestone. How selfish!

My mind was also in a state of conflict – family versus work and country. For many, it's not even a question that is entertained but I have never been one to walk away from agreements and career responsibilities. Unfortunately, there was an agreement – a plan forged several years ago that I felt compelled to honour. It's what sacrifice means – managing the stretch and tension between conflicting loyalties. There will be people out there who sit reading this in disbelief that any mother could leave her baby and young children for such a long time. I entertain that disbelief myself and had to detach myself from the voice in my head that asked: "What are you doing?"

I made another voice answer, to quash the first one: "It's happened. We have to learn to make it work."

The first week away on the ship was a waking nightmare. I missed my family as I'd never missed them before. Hormonal changes and the pain of engorged breasts plagued me as my body adjusted to the separation. I worried about my baby constantly and couldn't bear to dwell on what she was thinking. She probably felt I had died, or abandoned her. Would she even know me in three months?

I hated myself a little and repeatedly questioned the reasonableness of my decision to go through with the posting.

Is this really worth it?

What's the point of getting ahead in a career if you aren't happy or if your family is traumatised?

What if I'm doing irreparable damage to their development?

What if this ruins them long-term?

Somehow, I stumbled through each day.

Before we sailed to New Zealand, there was to be a planned sports day at HMAS *Creswell*, three hours south of Sydney.

"Sir, I'd like to ask for permission to meet my family at this time." I swallowed and sat taller, willing my Captain's compassion with every bone in my body. Mohamed could drive down with the kids. We could spend some time together.

The Captain was an amazing, supportive man who empathised with me immediately. "I know you're missing your family immensely. It must have been extremely hard leaving the newborn. I miss my clan so much, too. " A loving father and husband himself, he read my pain as though it was his own.

As much as Navy had evolved to have higher numbers of women at sea by that point, it was quite uncommon to have mothers of young babies on staff – let alone on deployment.

A very personable man, the Captain spent time getting to know each of his crew members personally. We had clicked over family and, suffice to say, soon became trusting colleagues as well as good friends. Our heartfelt discussions and the effort he made to support me emotionally when the ship's program dictated separation from family were not only appreciated but made me work even harder to deliver the best I could at all times. We were at similar stages in our lives and, in many ways, had aligned values. He would use the excuse of having to accompany me back to the ship after a night out with the crew to get away politely before things got too rowdy. I didn't drink and people knew that, but he didn't have a great excuse so I was a bit of a saviour.

"Well team, I had best leave with the Weapons Electrical Engineering Officer to make sure she gets back safely. Look out for each other and we'll see you tomorrow."

He was everything I admired in a leader and, just as there had been many superiors in the past whose actions and words had taught me how not to be, this Captain taught us all what worked through his behaviours and influence. I respected him immensely. It was the first time I understood what it meant for leaders to be lonely at the top – close enough to build respect and rapport, distant enough to maintain authority.

My posting was successful and effective on many fronts. I put all my previous training into action and led my department through almost every scenario a ship might expect while preparing for conflict or participating in diplomacy, search and rescue or border protection.

I looked forward to emails from Mohamed, who wrote regularly and diligently:

Shattering Identity Bias

We are all good here, keeping busy. Everything is going smoothly and the kids are doing very well at school. We caught up with the extended family on the weekend for a BBQ and the kids played all day with their cousins. They had a ball. I hope you are not too lonely. I will try to write often so you can feel like you are with us here.

He would always say he was okay because he had extended family and the kids to keep him occupied and happy. His position was to always worry about me as I was the one who was away and alone.

Mohamed came into his own during that period. He stood up to badgering from culturally-backward members of the community who told him he should divorce me and find another wife who better understood her place. His love, loyalty and unwavering devotion to both myself and the children were more than I could have asked for.

I also changed markedly during that posting. As the head of the Weapons Electrical Engineering Department, my confidence grew as I successfully implemented my experience and knowledge many times over. Morale had improved significantly within my department under my watch. Everything seemed to have fallen into place. I had been advised of an impending promotion to the next rank of commander. I felt very much loved by the crew (even those who were not too sure in the beginning). Plus, I was more than physically ripped, having lost all remnants of any fat storage after childbirth. My sacrifices in terms of my family had paid off; it had been hard but worth it.

The day we docked, I sat in the wardroom, waiting for Mohamed and the kids. I was so excited to be home.

An Officer of the Watch barged in, making me jump. "Man carrying baby and flowers with two other children in tow, portside, bearing 090," he announced. He was more excited than me, God bless him.

I ran to the gangway. There was my family, navigating their way beneath the tall crane fitted to the wharf against which the ship was berthed. The two oldest kids looked so tiny and Mohamed and the baby were particularly thin. Then, my son caught sight of me and his cheeky smile broadened as he pointed and ran.

"Mum. Mum!"

"Stop! Stop!" I screamed as a work vehicle barely missed him when he emerged from behind the crane.

He stopped immediately, petrified and very upset that his mother had shouted at him. Making things worse for him was probably the fact so many of the ship's crew were out on the upper decks watching the reunion of the young mum with her family. I suspect there was great interest in how I might react once I saw them; particularly the baby who I had left so young.

With my son crying and clinging to my legs and my oldest staring at me apprehensively, I kissed Mohamed on the cheek and went to grab my baby from his arms.

She pulled away, hanging on to Mohamed's shirt and burying her face in his shoulder. My heart broke – she didn't know me. Those first five months of life when we had never been separated, when I fed her day and night, changed her nappies and comforted her against my body were forgotten. I tried one more time to dislodge her from her dad's arms before letting her be. I felt bad enough about leaving her in the first place. I didn't deserve, nor could I demand, any affection from her at that point. I had abandoned her when she most needed me as a mother.

That night, she sat in bed between her father and me, staring at me in disbelief. I could read her mind through her hazel green eyes. Who are you? Why are you in my bed?

Shattering Identity Bias

Over the following week, I gave her lots of space and never came too close to her until she was ready to let me in again. It started with me feeding her and playing or helping with things she worked to master. It wasn't that long before she figured out that this 'Mum Thing' was not too bad at all. A month later, she was next on the ship on a planned family day. This time she clung to my uniform and grabbed my face smothering me with kisses as we traversed through the ship. Mohamed was out for the count as soon as the ship left the wharf. He slept in my rack, battling dreadful seasickness the whole day, while I showed the children around the vessel. The crew found them irresistible and I know our family reunion had brought everyone so much joy.

Section 2
Chief of Navy's Strategic Advisor on Islamic Cultural Affairs

Mona Shindy

Section 2: Introduction

❖

The end of my posting on HMAS *Melbourne* represented the end of my service at sea. From this point, I was to take on more enabling roles ashore, testing, supporting, maintaining and managing risks to our ships. I also spearheaded several critical roles and organisations both in Australia and abroad.

As a Commander, I performed duties as the Deputy Director of Navy's Test and Evaluation Organisation, assessing how well our platforms and supporting capabilities met the operational needs against which they were designed and delivered. I represented Australia as the Foreign Military Sales Liaison Officer charged with facilitating the effective integration of the US-sourced Aegis Combat System into the Navy's new destroyers having the F105 Spanish ship structural design.

From 2009 to 2012, Mohamed again put his career on hold to accompany me and support the family while I was stationed in Washington DC. Sacrifices we made were ultimately rewarded when I was promoted to the rank of Navy Captain in 2012 and appointed Director of the FFG System Program Office (FFGSPO).

Overall, my career to this point had been incredibly rewarding. I felt proud and privileged to be able to make very meaningful and impactful contributions to the effective operations and growth of the Australian Navy as one of its senior engineers. From leading the progress of new capabilities through government approvals and delivery, I had the great joy of project-managing the passage of many new ships and equipment into service. One of these ships was a replenishment oiler that my son was later to serve on as a trainee engineer himself.

Things were going well for us as a family. We had weaved our way home from the USA via a protracted journey through Europe. It was a wonderful experience for us all and a great firsthand learning opportunity for the children. Despite the challenges many families encounter stemming from travel, cultural adjustments and separation associated with military careers, the concurrent possibilities can be incredibly exciting and rewarding. Taking a winding road home was just one of many scenarios we would not necessarily have found ourselves enjoying if not for some of the career sacrifices made.

The kids were advanced beyond their peers academically – they had left behind some two-and-a-half years earlier – and Mohamed was fortunate enough to secure work within weeks of our return home. It was not at his previous level but was still within his field of expertise. With the children now progressing well in selective schools, our careers on track and the five of us able to enjoy the warmth and comfort of interactions with extended family and friendship networks again, Mohamed and I were very grateful for where we had landed.

As the FFGSPO Director, I was able to drive significant organisational reforms and establish new, innovative, performance-based contracts with industries that not only reduced waste but increased ship availability. With the ANZAC Class vessels being rotated through a capability upgrade program on the west coast of Australia, the FFGs I managed were now required to meet an increased operational tempo, despite increasing challenges with obsolescence and reliability due to their age.

I loved my job and the impact I knew I was making. Running a complex technical organisation meant I was able to bring together all the leadership skills I'd developed over many years, as well as the formal knowledge I'd gained through both my engineering and commerce degrees. Change management and project management were at the centre of everything I did but, without a doubt, the most rewarding aspect of what I did involved bringing my team along with me

– inspiring them to believe in the possibilities, helping them succeed and grow and celebrating the significant and collective wins we made together.

I felt respected at work and had established strong relationships with a wide network of peers, senior mentors, staff and industry partners. My work and performance record meant I was able to gain the trust and confidence of senior leadership as well as of those with whom I interacted daily. I was very much one of the team and, aside from my skin colour, I was not too noticeably different from the majority of officers at my rank level. There were also a lot more women now visible in positions of authority and significant responsibility.

So, despite some of the earlier challenges I had worked through to gain acceptance as both a gender and a cultural minority, I knew my patience and resilience had paid off to this point and that Navy had made inroads during my career. These inroads required many adjustments from all involved as they strove to accommodate a comfortable middle ground, where individual differences could be absorbed while still meeting all military and operational objectives.

For a long time, I remained guarded about how much I would let others see of my life. Self-preservation is a natural and powerful instinct that often deters even the most courageous. Letting others into my personal world, especially as part of a minority group, wasn't ever easy for me and was something I both thought and worried about a lot. So, it was really strange for me when I was asked to take on a secondary role that would require me to teach colleagues about my Islamic faith traditions and to implement initiatives designed to increase the appeal of the navy as an employer of choice for Muslim youth. The navy had successfully tackled a number of diversity and inclusion challenges head-on and change had occurred, despite the noticeable resistance and pain.

I also truly believed, and still do, that diverse perspectives informed by different inputs are what enriches communities. It is diversity of thought that sparks new ideas and innovation. Meshing perspectives and avoiding conclusions drawn primarily from homogenous silos serves to educate and strengthen organisational and community capability. It may not always provide the most comfortable or unanimously-liked group settings, but it is necessary to achieve the best performance and outcomes. Diversity is what makes each and every one of us individual and special. It is what we offer to the world to inform collective growth and what gives us personal meaning. It is important and the freedom to express it is liberating.

My experiences to this point had taught me people are much more similar than different. I'd always felt that the more we can open ourselves up to looking, learning and sharing, the more we are able to not only begin to understand and appreciate individual differences but to celebrate them as things that enrich us all.

Those who really know me would also attest to the abundance of my optimism. Some would even say 'hopeful naivety in the face of imminent threat'. I had reached the point where I dearly wanted to do a good job for Navy and make a tangible and lasting difference.

With this perspective and this overarching belief, I cautiously agreed to be involved in this new program, taking the helm as a secondary role. I wanted to give back as much as I could to an organisation I loved and a community I deeply cared for. I also wanted to make an important difference for minorities who would follow after I was long retired and gone. I felt a real responsibility to do whatever I could to ensure some of the negative experiences I had throughout my career were not endured by my son and others like him. I was determined to effect change, regardless of the challenges. I trusted that the senior leaders, having identified and understood a need for further cultural reform, would stand by me and offer all the support required to achieve success for their proposed new initiative. The new tasking itself gave me hope that there was an appetite for change and a desire to really tackle needed inclusion and diversity reforms. I had every confidence that, as part of the team, my physical and psychological safety would be assured.

Chapter 1:
An Awakening of Self (2013)

It was in the second year of my posting, running the Fast Frigate System Program Office (FFGSPO) and supporting the upkeep of the Navy's Adelaide Class frigates, that I was startled to receive a direct phone call from above.

"This is the Deputy Chief of Navy, Mona. How are you doing?"

Why would the second-in-charge of Navy be calling me directly? Had I done something wrong? Was there a new operational tasking from the government that required me to ready a vessel in deep maintenance at the rush?

After overcoming the short paralysis generated by my surprise, I responded with an obedient, "Yes, Sir. How can I help?"

"The Senior Leadership Team have been discussing ways we can make Navy more inclusive. The Chief of Navy already has a Women's Strategic Adviser but is looking to expand the range of advisors available to him. We are standing up an Indigenous Affairs Adviser and another who can provide insights on how best to support our LGBTQI community. I was wondering if you would be up for taking on the collateral duty of Navy's Strategic Adviser on Islamic Cultural Affairs?"

I was taken aback by his matter-of-fact tone and the strangeness of such a proposal. There was such a small number of Muslims currently serving in the Australian Navy and even more broadly within the entire defence force. I asked why there was a need for an adviser.

"That is the very point, Mona," he said. "We have to start somewhere and work out how to attract and retain the most capable Australians from diverse backgrounds to deliver the right capability effect into the future. We are competing with the mining industry and others who do a great job presenting themselves as employers of choice to the finite talent pool."

But why an Islamic Cultural Adviser? It seemed so specific and narrow in scope. I had not fully explored all plausible reasons in my thinking when the Deputy Chief elaborated further.

"When the Senior Leadership Team were exploring the options, we discussed a range of minorities. We noted how far Navy has come through the implementation of New Generation Navy. Many within the group sighted the strong inroads made and attested to the navy of today being very different to the one they had joined as young officers. They talked about how women were now well integrated and how policies and behaviours had changed, such that being openly gay was no longer an issue in our Navy. There is a lot for us to be proud of," he declared.

He went on to say that, further into the discussion, the senior leaders began to feel challenged by their own attitudes. "It became increasingly clear that there was still much work to be done. When they were asked about how they would feel if a Muslim family moved in next door to theirs … well, let's say their biases were clear through the silence in the room."

He casually communicated this last point, seemingly oblivious to the possibility that it might cut me somehow. After all, I was a proud

Australian Muslim serving under the command of these leaders. He went on to explain the Chief of Navy had decided that by tackling the most difficult of issues – acceptance and accommodation of Muslims – Navy would develop the necessary structural reforms to support all diverse minorities.

"Navy understands that cultural reform initiatives require ongoing effort and focus to ensure the benefits are meaningful and enduring," he said.

"Sir, I'm willing to help in whatever way I can," I heard myself say. What other option did I have? I was not in the habit of blowing off senior officers when they asked me to do something and, in some ways, I felt flattered and privileged to be asked. I was even impressed that the senior leaders appeared to be serious about effecting necessary reform.

Throughout my career, I had always silently craved such a reform and thought it to be more important than ever now, given the elevated negative national and international commentary about Muslims, stemming from associations being drawn to the growing ISIS threat.

"I appreciate your understanding and assistance, Mona." He advised I would soon be sent an instrument of appointment, which would explain the scope and duties associated with this additional role. Then he cleared his throat. "If Navy were to change the uniform dress code to allow you to wear a hijab," he said, "would you be willing to take up that option?" It was framed as an afterthought, although I was quite sure it wasn't.

I had occasionally fantasised about being free to wear the hijab in uniform and openly show all I valued but it had never occurred to me that it might one day become a possibility. I was in shock at his question. Intuitively, for most of my life I had chosen not to wear a hijab in any public setting, simply so as not to have to deal with the prejudice and discrimination I knew it would attract.

"Yes," I said immediately. I gave the proposal no thought or reflection – very unlike me.

Knowing the navy environment well, I had no reason to believe things would be different here; even if the senior leaders sanctioned and supported the initiative. This change would be significant and difficult. I almost felt a sense of responsibility to help facilitate the proposal, particularly given people were going out of their way to do something for me, and others like me.

It was not long before the instrument of appointment was emailed to me. I read it initially with some level of cynicism, knowing that such talk had previously always been about merely demonstrating expected alignment with Government policy on equal opportunity – usually on paper but not in practice. For years, I had listened to values being espoused and drilled into our people, then left behind in the training room without being implemented in the work environment.

As I read, my gaze became more focused. A new feeling of relief, perhaps even hope, stirred in my gut. Here was a document, signed by the Chief of Navy, that talked about enhancing organisational capability. It wasn't some feel-good mush about making staff more welcome but argued a real business need to create a stronger and more effective Navy organisation.

Several broad objectives had been documented. Some related to education about and accommodation of Islamic cultural practices. It sought to increase awareness of cultural sensitivities for Australian Navy personnel when engaged with other navies that had a significant Islamic workforce. It was all about increasing Navy capability through education, inclusion and harnessing the diversity of thought. The appointment called for the development and implementation of initiatives to better meet the needs of Muslims with the view to attracting and retaining valuable talent from that segment of Australian society. It sought to break down structural barriers and present Navy as an inclusive and progressive employer of choice.

I sat back from my computer and breathed out slowly. How refreshing it was to read something so forward-looking that spoke to issues I thought would never be broached by my Navy, certainly not in my lifetime. I looked back at the screen. Yet here it was. Evidence that, for me at the time, proved the Navy senior leaders were serious and prepared to act on what I had always felt was just a symbolic and tokenistic narrative.

Still sceptical but hopeful, I allowed myself to drink a little of the Kool-Aid. I needed to respond to the Chief of Navy in relation to this new appointment and took great care to ensure my correspondence aptly captured my feelings and thoughts at the time. I wanted the Vice Admiral to gain some good insights from the very first interaction I had with him.

Mona Shindy

CN Sir,

1. I have received my letter of appointment as Navy Strategic Adviser on Islamic Cultural Affairs. I welcome this appointment as a wonderful opportunity to contribute constructively to your stated objectives within the letter of appointment. Throughout my life, I have often felt like a bridge straddling communities, separated by what is still a distinct and firm boundary line propped up through misunderstanding and misconceptions on both sides and concerns and aversions fuelled by fear and uncertainty. I hope to be able to assist in further bridging this divide by informing discussions and creating increased understanding and cohesion for the better good of all concerned.

2. For the Australian Defence Force (ADF), the potential benefits that this opportunity presents could be profound. I see that significant inroads could be made in the following areas:

a. The furthering of New Generation Navy (NGN) cultural reform objectives aimed at promoting the benefits of inclusiveness and diversity. This will ensure we can create and nurture the type of environment and behaviours we need to attract and retain talent from all areas of our multi-cultural society.

b. Through a continued and deliberate focus on identifying and removing barriers to recruitment, Navy can increase its appeal as an employer of choice for all Australians, thereby attracting a balanced mix of recruits whose numbers and proportions align with the constituent percentages of the broad Australian demographic. There is a large untapped recruiting opportunity from within a relatively young and fast-growing Australian Muslim community. As a mother, I believe I am well placed to influence those most likely to impact a young adult's career choices, namely the parents. This reality is even more relevant for the Australian Islamic community, where parental advice is very influential.

My feedback from Muslim mothers and teachers from Islamic schools the Navy has previously targeted is that the messaging about Australia's military operations abroad in predominantly Muslim nations has at times been offensive, often delivered by Navy representatives who have little or no understanding of the cultural and religious sensitivities. It is all in the marketing.

c. Improved rapport and relations between Australia and many of its neighbours who have predominantly Islamic populations and live by Islamic principles and value systems.

3. For the Australian Islamic community, I believe the opportunities this appointment could provide are also very valuable and significant. In an environment where the media images of Muslims are by far more negative than positive, any opportunity to present the other face of Muslims' contribution to Australia, which is where the vast majority of Australian Muslims sit and operate, can only be a good thing for community cohesion and respectful integration. This is important to me personally on several levels:

a. Having had the great privilege of serving my country for over 24 years in the Defence arena and the opportunity to demonstrate in very practical and tangible ways that Muslims can effectively integrate and do good things; I feel I almost have a duty to give back to the community that raised me and gave me the fundamental building blocks and character traits with which I live and interact as a citizen and leader within the Australian Defence Force (ADF).

b. As a mother of young Australian Muslims who I know have often felt alienated, embarrassed, vilified and ridiculed over many years of negative reporting and media messaging, I also feel a strong sense of obligation and responsibility to help make their lives easier and happier. This is basically the mission of any mother who wants her children to have satisfying lives and to feel well included and valued in the only society and country they know and love as their own. My personal experience with my own children, I know is not foreign to any other Muslim family in Australia.

c. The appointment also affords me the opportunity to act as a positive role model for young Australian Muslims. A prevailing "victim mentality" is a strong and real affliction clearly evident within Australian Islamic society as a whole. It is that sense of helplessness and fear of trying to integrate that stifles many young Muslims who are simply convinced that Australian society rejects them because they are Muslim. This not only excludes a career in the ADF from their thinking but also sometimes drives them to unsavoury elements that operate on the fringes of Islamic society, actively seeking to recruit impressionable youngsters easily convinced that non-Muslims have an agenda against them. The most effective way to combat such undesirable influences is through the creation of real opportunities, careers and avenues for integration and contribution. Young Muslims need to feel and see that they can and do belong. That said, the ADF must also ensure that we really provide those opportunities. I cannot tell you how many capable, bright, highly qualified young Australian Muslims I have encouraged to apply to the ADF throughout my career, who have come back to me after being rejected through the recruitment process convinced that they were not wanted because their names were Mohamed, Mahmoud, Bilal or Ahmed. I must admit, based on what I know of those young Muslims who applied and what I know of many who do successfully get through the recruitment process, their cynicism may well be justified.

4. The appointment as Navy Strategic Advisor on Islamic and Cultural Affairs must through necessity remain a secondary collateral duty to my primary current role as FFGSPO Director. The SPO Director's role, as I know you are well acquainted, is complex and highly demanding. It draws heavily on my skills as an Engineer, business professional and change agent. In an exceedingly resource-constrained environment where FFGs are being relied on to carry much of the Major Surface Ships' (MSS) operational obligations, while simultaneously preparing to decommission (efficiently and cost consciously) as the Destroyers come on-line, the work tempo is gruelling and constant requiring significant innovation, detailed planning and analysis.

5. With that backdrop of my daily reality, I propose that I will be able to commit one day each month to meet your objectives in relation to the "Navy Strategic Advisor on Islamic Cultural Affairs" role. I envisage initially that I will accompany you to meet with Australian Islamic leaders to explore opportunities to further your agenda for interaction with the Muslim community. I will also make myself available to give presentations at community gatherings/forums and at educational institutions. I will continue to work with Director General Logistics to introduce female Islamic dress into the Navy by developing appropriate uniform designs meeting religious clothing observance requirements. I will develop these uniform designs for your approval over the coming 12 months. It remains my intention to eventually dress in Islamic uniform attire, but as discussed with DCN, the timing for me personally will revolve around when I am able to complete my Islamic obligation of Hajj and when I feel I have sufficient time professionally and the emotional energy to handle and adequately respond to the likely level of interest and questioning that such a move may attract, both internally in the work environment and potentially externally through media interest.

6. To adequately prepare myself to be successful in this new role, I believe I will need to complete "Media Awareness Training" and understand who it is I will need to consult with and seek permission from before engaging externally outside Navy when opportunities arise.

7. I will also need continued senior management support to have the freedom to try new things besides performing my normal day job. I look forward to being able to contribute positively to the objectives of this new role.

I have the honour to be Sir.

Your obedient servant
M. SHINDY
CAPT, RAN

I had always been a devout Muslim. I was disciplined about praying five times a day, fasting the holy month of Ramadan each year and giving in charity. It was natural and logical for me to believe in the existence of one omnipotent creator deserving of worship. My interest in and passion for science and mathematics only solidified and reinforced this strong belief. Our marvellous universe, with its intricate complexity and perfect proportions, has always been sufficient evidence for me. Revealed centuries before being broadly accepted by acclaimed scientists, the scientific facts described in the holy Quran have further supported my conviction.

However, despite this, when I was appointed as Navy's Strategic Adviser on Islamic Cultural Affairs, I suddenly felt ill-prepared to be providing advice on all things relating to Islamic beliefs and culture or to compare and contrast if asked about other faith traditions. This triggered a self-imposed tasking to read widely and deeply. Born a Sunni Muslim, I had a rudimentary knowledge of the various sects and historical events that shaped the Muslim world. I had even less knowledge of the violent and repugnant terrorist groups who claimed legitimacy via a self-proclaimed association with Islam. I had only read the Quran about three times by this stage in my life. This was via three different English translations, which cannot be characterised as the authentic message originally delivered in poetic, classic Arabic. I had read several books documenting the Islamic Hadith and Prophet Muhammad's conduct (Sunna) and one or two on Islamic history. My exploration of other faiths was even less thorough.

Through my reading and research, my beliefs and devotion grew stronger. I found a great deal to be impressed by and proud of. I read about Islam's early history, the persecution suffered by its first adherents, the oppressive practices it sought to dismantle and the changes it drove in societies. I read of both male and female leaders and warriors, of scientists and mathematicians and of critical thought that fuelled advancements in philosophy, art and social systems of governance and justice. I learned about the different groups who claim an association with the religion of Islam and sought to understand how and why their traditions varied to those I had been taught through my birth lineage. I read more deeply about other faiths and spiritual traditions, noting similarities and differences to Islam.

If not for this new appointment as a Strategic Adviser, it is unlikely I'd have ever sought to educate myself further about the religions of the world. Religion had always been uncomplicated to me and remains so to this day. It is a simple and direct spiritual connection with the creator and nothing more. It has always seemed unimportant to me how that connection is expressed. The important issue for me was that all people have the freedom to express their beliefs, or lack of them, in whatever way they feel to be most comfortable and appropriate.

As I read further, I experienced an awakening of self. I knew I'd been self-censoring for years. I'd allowed the views, prejudice and behaviours of others to affect how I expressed and represented myself. I'd always hidden my spiritual identity. My reasoning was informed by a strong desire to just get on, fit in and belong to the majority – those who dominated the circles in which I lived and worked and those who had decision-making power over my inclusion and opportunities. It was always easier to adopt the practices and norms preferred by almost all around me and to agree with the dominant views and prevailing narrative. I knew that people responded better to those who were just like themselves, who they found more relatable and, as such, more likeable.

In the main, shared human values make assimilation possible and palatable, providing the easiest path to acceptance and success.

For so long, this had been enough for me. I had been willing to suppress aspects of myself and keep quiet rather than offer an alternate view or understanding on why or how the world could be interpreted differently. I'd felt satisfied with being able to progress professionally, pay my bills and help raise my family.

The more I read and reflected, the more apparent it became that I was allowing my true self to be compromised and seen as second class in my own country.

I questioned myself constantly.

How could you have done this, Mona? How could you aid and prolong mediocrity when it came to the navy and the nation being able to capitalise on Australia's rich diversity of perspectives. We could and should do better.

I did not want my children to live the same repressed life I now realised I had allowed myself to live.

I had arrived at a point in my life where I, as part of the minority, could be more confident about picking and choosing the norms that worked best for me. I knew some would appear strange to others – namely, the majority who still had so much influence on how comfortable, or otherwise, my life would be.

With my organisation's stated support, I finally felt I had permission to express all I valued and all that combined to define my full self.

Mona Shindy

Chapter 2:
Cultural Reform - Not Everyone's Idea of a Good Thing (2013-2015)

Believing was one thing but summoning the courage to put myself out there was a gradual and significant struggle. I took the less risky steps first and worked diligently to meet the Vice Admiral's vision. I organised and accompanied him on visits to Islamic community leaders. I developed education materials and delivered many information sessions on Islamic cultural practices to colleagues and to ships' companies as part of their pre-deployment briefs. I engaged with schools that had large numbers of Muslim students and established a Navy Cadet Unit in Western Sydney.

Setting up structural pathways to introduce Navy as a career option for Muslims was accompanied by work that was necessary to attract and retain the right type of talent. Dietary options within the messes, prayer facilities and the removal of barriers that unwittingly restricted opportunities to participate in faith traditions were some of the initiatives I tackled to ensure the needs of all personnel were reasonably accommodated. I worked with the Navy Chaplains on the Chief of Navy's request to secure the first-ever Muslim chaplain for the Australian Navy.

I rattle these accomplishments off today as though they just fell into place but, in truth, most eventuated only after much resistance and significant pain for many, including myself. This pain came from many sources. Some felt discomfort about needing to make space in policy and processes for what was perhaps seen as a small insignificant minority. "Lots of work and cost, for what? We are busy enough as it is," was a comment I heard when exploring hijab design options for the uniform. Often, I sensed that some people felt space for others would mean less opportunity for themselves. Regularly, there seemed to be artificial barriers presented that implied change was going to be more difficult and slower than it needed to be.

For me, the pain came from a constant need to respectfully and tactfully address the roadblocks, while, at the same time, dealing with the emotional impact of numerous discussions and negotiations where I sometimes felt devalued, disrespected and even rejected.

Training Ship Australia is the name that was finally given to the cadet unit in Western Sydney. Proposed by one of the young lieutenants who worked for me at the FFGSPO, 'Australia' was the namesake of the first Australian Navy flagship, HMAS *Australia*. It was the tradition that cadet units would reflect the name of a current or previously serving Naval vessel. Most cadet units would choose names that matched the localities in which they were housed. With TS Sydney already taken, the name TS Australia appeared to be quite fitting for the new cadet unit established in Lidcombe and positioned ideally to service multicultural Australia.

Almost as soon as the name was suggested, a campaign within the broader cadet community took off to block the name 'Australia' from being taken by the apparently 'undeserving Muslims'. Some cadet community members were outraged at the brazen audacity of this subset of Australians associating themselves with the name 'Australia'.

"Perhaps a different name would be more fitting to describe the locality at which the cadet unit is housed."

"Cadet units have also started moving away from using previous ship names," the Flotilla Commander advised.

"Australia has never been used before," was another piece of advice I received from a fellow cadet unit Commanding Officer who clearly had not done any research about a unit that had been around for a short period in the 1940s.

"You guys will probably just fizzle out anyway." One of the central training staff thought it appropriate to throw in that comment as the proposed name of the cadet unit was being socialised.

The National Commander for Navy Cadets led the protest. "The name Australia has sacrosanct reverence," he insisted. "You will need to choose an alternate name."

It was at a time in Australia when almost everything about Muslims was being politicised. The media headline in The Australian – *We'll fight radical Islam for 100 years, says ex-army head Peter Leahy* – was indicative of the media focus at the time. New counterterrorism laws were being introduced and sold under the Government of the day as necessary to protect the nation from those 'scary' Muslims. One image I vividly remember was of the Prime Minister standing in front of six Australian flags at a press conference to announce the introduction of new initiatives relating to 'the war on terror'.

It was an era where so much was occurring that served to marginalise and demonise the Muslim community. There was a clear trend of increased Islamophobia attacks. There was a senate inquiry set up to look at third-party certification of food and although it was supposed to cover all categories, including organically and genetically-modified and Kosher foods, the overwhelming focus of the debate and directed hatred was related to Halal, which, incidentally, means 'lawful' in the Islamic context. There was political commentary and inquiry into how Muslims parented children and into the clothes they chose to wear. Muslims were on the outer and were literally being *othered* every single day. With so much baggage and symbolism impregnating the national psyche, it was inevitable this would also impact views and attitudes within the ADF and the Navy cadet community. The struggle experienced in naming the cadet unit gives a strong insight into just how hard it was to affect any change within the ADF at the time.

Initially, I quickly sought to avert any conflict by bowing to the majority view – something I'd instinctively done my whole life. It was the only approach that I knew would work and allow me to continue doing my job. I had learned to diminish so many aspects of myself over the years. I considered the names TS Western Sydney and TS Parramatta and noted them as potential alternatives in a brief I wrote to the Vice Admiral. I described our progress and then I informed him of the resistance I was confronting. Previously, I would not have mentioned any drama encountered in a brief such as this, but the situation angered me and I felt it important I advise the Chief of Navy about what I knew to be outright prejudice.

The brief was returned to me with the Vice Admiral's green pen scratchings over it.

Sacrosanct? Rubbish! TS Australia it is!

I still remember the warm delight I felt reading these words. I'd always admired the Vice Admiral but this small gesture made me respect him even more and convinced me he was genuine about leading cultural reform.

Shattering Identity Bias

There were many items on the agenda for me in this role, including halal meal options on our ships and bases and educational briefings on cultural sensitivities, but the first one I was tasked with tackling was the issue of chaplains.

Along with the external Religious Advisory Committee to the Services (RACS), I suspected the Navy Chaplains were perhaps the group that felt most threatened and uncertain about the Chief of Navy appointing a Strategic Adviser on Islamic Cultural Affairs. With RACS, they saw themselves as having sole responsibility for advising on all issues pertinent to any faith tradition. The fact that they were comprised exclusively of Christian and Jewish clergy, reaching back to an Affiliated Representative Committee (ARC) where other faith groups were represented symbolically, meant they no longer provided a suitable structure to reflect the interests and beliefs of all who served or might consider serving from the broad Australian demographic.

An outdated policy served as the basis for the arguments they presented for maintaining the status quo and excluding Muslims and other minority groups from becoming Navy Chaplains. This policy stated that a certain number of religious adherents must be serving before they were entitled to tailored pastoral care within the ranks.

It was the classic chicken and egg scenario. Inclusive services would certainly increase recruitment and retention of a more complete range of Australians but these would be denied until an arbitrary quota of serving personnel was reached. The further irony was that rule did not seem to apply to the Jewish grouping who had smaller numbers serving than Muslims or to the actual majority 'non-religious' grouping who would prefer pastoral care to be provided by secular professionals with skills in disciplines such as philosophy, psychology or social work.

A major concern highlighted by the Vice Admiral was that despite the Australian Navy's frequent interactions with other navies with a high Muslim representation, our people had little idea about cross-cultural implications. As such, one of his goals was education and his first objective was to gain engagement with the Grand Mufti of Australia to discuss initiatives he wanted to pursue – one of which was the appointment of a Muslim chaplain for Navy.

The Vice Admiral's proposal was something he told me the organisation had grappled with for a while. "The chaplains previously tasked to investigate the proposal had never been able to progress it to realisation," he said.

Now that I'd been tasked to take it forward in my capacity as his Strategic Adviser on Islamic Cultural Affairs, I'd unwittingly become an instant target for those who did not agree with the proposal.

"The Islamic Community has too many different sects who can't agree on which Imam should be put forward," one Navy Chaplain advised.

"Muslims have different ways and requirements for assessing someone competent to be an Imam or chaplain. There appears to be no structured appointing authority as we have in the Christian tradition," another proclaimed.

Gaining an appointment with the Grand Mufti was not easy, and I had many failed attempts to align calendars in 2013.

Early interactions I had with the Grand Mufti's office, where I explained the Vice Admiral's intent and purpose for a requested engagement generated considerable activity within the Islamic religious community, led by the Australian National Imams Council (ANIC), to understand the chaplaincy requirements and to identify a suitable Muslim chaplain candidate. I helped organise several meetings with the hierarchy in the Navy Chaplaincy Branch, Defence Force Recruiting and RACS representatives.

In the months that marched on before the Vice Admiral could meet with the Grand Mufti, apprehension and resistance from the existing RACS and Navy Chaplaincy community was growing. Many reasons were provided as to why the prospect of a Muslim chaplain could not be supported, including assertions that there were structural and legal restrictions – difficult to address through government decisions – that necessitated a Muslim representative being a member of RACS, so that person could nominate a suitable chaplain for Navy.

The uncomfortable rumblings were also filtering through to the Vice Admiral, who expressed his concern that existing Defence religious advisers were questioning the necessity of my role and suggesting it was seen as more religious than cultural.

It was around the same time that social media chatter started appearing about the 'new threat' that was now apparently unsettling a number of religious and special interest advocacy groups. That threat was specifically identified as 'no other than one Captain Mona Shindy', an 'externally demure and unassuming character who secretly had sinister motivations'.

I had never paid much notice to this kind of thing, mainly because I did not spend a lot of time perusing social media and had no significant presence online. I was aware that trolling took place but never understood the profound negative impact it could have on an individual until I was targeted.

Notwithstanding the decades of loyal and dedicated military service I had under my belt and my well-reported professional credibility, these trolls still found ways to spread lies and whip up hatred that reverberated from one echo chamber to another. From right-wing extremist groups painting me as a 'sleeper' and 'infiltrator' with likely ties to terrorist groups to advocacy groups and political nationalist groups campaigning on platforms of intolerance, I was increasingly mocked, vilified and ridiculed.

My public profile had been slowly growing, with Navy excited to showcase the initiatives it was pursuing in the area of diversity and inclusion reforms. Despite the pockets of negativity, which I tried very hard to ignore, most of the reporting was positive and supportive. The Vice Admiral encouraged me to give several interviews for media, both internal and external to Defence. The work I was leading was featured in newspaper articles, magazines, community interest pieces on mainstream television and, when opportunities were presented, to international audiences such as the International Fleet Review that took place in October 2013. The Fleet Review was part of the celebrations to commemorate the 100th anniversary of the entry of the first Royal Australian Navy fleet into Sydney Harbour in 1913. I even cracked out my rudimentary Arabic skills for community radio to reach migrant parents who could influence and encourage their children to consider a naval career.

When it came to the Navy Chaplaincy community and leadership, body language and inaction often said more than words. What was generally presented as collegiate and cooperative interest and support on the surface, often masked a deep underlying apprehension and resistance to change or accommodation of non-Christian-Judaic faith traditions, particularly when it came to decision-making or influencing positions. I had certainly captured the attention of the group in a number of ways: while working with them to implement the Vice Admiral's objectives in relation to securing a Muslim chaplain for Navy; when participating in their workshops as the invited guest speaker; and through a growing public interest in both Navy's work around diversity and inclusion and my own personal story.

Two significant interactions I had at the time with Navy Chaplains will remain with me forever.

The first related to a short address and the crafting of a 'prayer for diversity' I was asked to deliver at the beautiful St Mary's Cathedral in

Sydney during the International Fleet Review. It was to be part of an inclusive service that incorporated prayers from many faith traditions represented in the different international navies present at the event. As with all such services in Navy, the Chaplains were asked to coordinate.

The toing-and-froing between me and the organisers leading up to the event was painful. It started with them providing me with words they had already written and wanted me to say.

> *Attached is the prayer you can read out. The words acknowledge all the diverse faith groups that will be present.*

Not only did I find this particularly arrogant but it reminded me of just how much Navy's Chaplains had, at best, not considered and, at worst, devalued my beliefs and spiritual needs throughout my entire career. I have always been very respectful of all Navy traditions, including the religious ceremonies that were always Christian in content and message. I never once made a fuss about having to attend compulsory services during my early career under training or while participating in parades and ceremonies. I would listen quietly, very conscious not to offend or distract from proceedings where others were engaged in worship and heartfelt reflection. In fact, it would be fair to say I probably got more out of the Christian ceremonies and enjoyed listening to the sermons more than most in attendance. After all, the commonalities between the Christian and Muslim faith traditions are numerous.

It annoyed me that the one time I was finally given an opportunity to express myself and my prayer in my own way, I was again being told what to do. I would send through the words I wanted to say and many attempts were made to curtail them but I persisted. It was an occasion where I felt strongly about standing my ground and that I deserved to be treated with the same respect I had always shown to others when they expressed their beliefs in their own way.

The coordinating Chaplain and I eventually landed on a set of words I was comfortable with and that fit well within my allocated speaking time. Given the large number of Muslims that would be present, I indicated I would start with a short Arabic recitation from the Quran, the Fatiha. This is the opening verse of the Muslim holy book, something Muslims recite daily and would find highly relatable, and that would also showcase the core of Islamic belief to non-Muslims once translated. It would take no longer than one minute and would be a highly symbolic, respectful and inclusive prelude to the English section of my address where I would ask God to keep all our navies' mariners safe until their return home.

"No, no. You can't recite the verse from the Quran as it will probably place you over time. I won't include it in the proceedings or run-sheet," advised the event coordinator. Only the words I would say in English were to be placed in the proceedings pamphlet that would be handed out to all attending the church ceremony.

On the day, when it was my turn to speak, my heart started racing and I even experienced a slightly panicked shortness of breath. Despite its omission from the proceedings pamphlet, I had resolved to start with my chosen verse from the holy Quran. As I began, I could see the confusion in the audience as they searched the pamphlet for what I was saying. Senior dignitaries sat, attentively engaged in the front rows and the clergy quietly looked at each other. I didn't care. I was careful with my pronunciation, deliberate with my emphasis and so very proud to be sharing something so dear to me with everyone in that cathedral.

I followed my recitation directly with an English translation before finally getting to the words in the proceedings pamphlet. I knew my piece was highly impactful and very different to anything anyone had ever heard during such a Navy service. On completion, I left the cathedral, walking at a pace straight down between the pews in search of my husband. I avoided making eye contact with the many attendees who seemed to be trying to engage with me in some way.

Finally, I made it out through the elaborate rear doors and found Mohamed waiting for me on the steps. "That was great, Mona! You did really well and I could see people were very engaged when you spoke," he said. Instantly, I was comforted that I had done what I set out to do.

We mingled for a while and were approached by a myriad of attendees who were very gracious with their words of support.

"That was a beautiful and perfectly pronounced recitation from the Quran you gave. May God bless you," an Egyptian Coptic Orthodox priest said in Arabic as he passed by.

"Thank you for the beautiful prayer," an Indonesian Officer said to me, his hand affectionately placed on Mohamed's shoulder. Mohamed has always been a little shy and reserved but is always ready to show up and support me in whatever way he can. This situation was no different. With nothing at all said, Mohamed reciprocated with a warm smile and a simple nod of the head.

It wasn't long before I noticed the Vice Admiral weaving his way through the crowd; a smile on his face I can only describe as beaming. "Thank you so much for coming," he said, giving Mohamed's hand a firm shake. He turned to me. "Everyone is talking about your prayer and how different it was from anything they had heard before." He looked very pleased with the feedback he'd received and was clearly delighted that inroads for greater inclusion and understanding were visibly being made.

On the way home, Mohamed and I chatted about the day. I felt great and was very pleased I was able to share something so dear and personal to me.

"That is the first time in my career I have been able to worship naturally. To actually be seen as a serving Muslim by the whole ADF community. To speak from the heart and give totally of myself. It feels wonderful.

How good is it that Navy is serious about including everyone," I said to Mohamed.

"Yep, that bloke is doing really good things," Mohamed acknowledged the Vice Admiral. I could see in his expression that he also felt more included than ever before.

The second significantly memorable encounter with the Navy Chaplain community of the time occurred some twelve months later in the clothing store at HMAS *Kuttabul*.

I had been wearing hijab and an adjusted Navy uniform designed to meet Islamic dress requirements for about one month and, while waiting in line to be served, was confronted by a young chaplain. "What kind of uniform is that!" he said in a manner both aggressive and insubordinate.

This was only the beginning.

The discussion progressed into a more critical dialogue. "I think the introduction of an Islamic chaplain will dilute the way Christian chaplains can run services," he declared, his manner somewhat agitated. "I am really concerned about Christians no longer being able to fully follow their normal processes or use all their meaningful language and phrases of worship."

Despite being shocked by his brazen and disrespectful tone – something I had never experienced so directly from a subordinate at any stage in my career – I remained calm, giving him the benefit of the doubt in relation to his intentions.

"I am sure all your concerns can be addressed to ensure inclusion for all and no dilution for anyone," I said. The exchange was over very quickly given I had reached the front of the queue and it was my turn to be served.

He turned away and left almost as quickly as he had appeared. He had seemed genuinely worried and I could empathise with how important it was for him to be able to practise his religion authentically and freely, however, I felt uncomfortable that he had made such a spectacle in front of all within the store. I was embarrassed. People were ogling me. I could see they were disturbed by the rudeness of the encounter and I suspect they were a little upset to see me face such open prejudice and distaste.

I know I hadn't effectively allayed the young man's fears and that I was unlikely to, no matter what amount of time I had spent talking in that particular setting. There was venom in his eyes and I was the enemy in his mind.

※

When the Vice Admiral finally met the Grand Mufti in April 2014, the key outcome he sought was, as previously mentioned, Muslim community assistance to identify a suitable Islamic chaplain for Navy. There was also a clear intention from the government, with the Assistant Defence Minister, the honourable Stuart Robert speaking in parliament of the plans for greater religious diversity for Navy chaplaincy.

After the meeting, however, things 'went quiet'. The president of ANIC maintained periodic contact with me over several months, seeking updates on which of the provided applications Navy would like to progress to interview. There was confusion as to why Navy was offering no response in relation to the candidates who had been put forward as potentially suitable chaplains. I worked hard to manage expectations and explain internal Defence processing times, all while feeling very uncomfortable about the internal politics I knew were at play and were responsible for the inaction.

I found myself managing many important relationships inside and outside Navy with limited support. Through circumstance, I became the meat in the sandwich and was expected by all stakeholders – external and internal – to somehow sort everything out in an environment where things were off and running before adequate internal consultation had occurred, roadblocks addressed, risks adequately mitigated and buy-in secured.

It would be fair to say there came a point when Islamic community leaders concluded they were not being engaged in a genuine way.

"This is a big change for Navy," I would explain. "It is never straightforward to put in place all that is necessary to create a new position and prepare for induction and training."

"After all the requests for assistance to find a suitable Muslim chaplain, it makes no sense that it should now be taking so long to get a reply. The applicants keep ringing me to enquire about the selection process," the head of ANIC explained, clearly frustrated with the evasive stalling.

I did advise the Vice Admiral of the growing frustration and disappointment communicated by the Muslim community leaders and the understanding I had that there might be an approach made to the government. He listened carefully but offered no response to this advice.

It was ultimately a direct approach made by ANIC to the Minister of Defence that resulted in a Muslim nominee being put forward to the government for a seat on RACS. The nominated person was eventually appointed to RACS and it was he who nominated a suitable candidate as the first Muslim Reserve Chaplain for Navy.

It was a milestone I had thought was unlikely to happen, given the very visible resistance from those who felt threatened by the prospect and from those who would normally be tasked to make it happen. For years, it had been clear an intervention was needed and it was finally made by the Vice Admiral when he appointed me as an independent adviser, tasked to unpack artificial barriers. Ultimately, the change came through political intervention when the facts could no longer reasonably be ignored.

Such a significant reform never comes easily.

By this stage in Navy's cultural inclusion journey, the first appointed RACS Muslim representative had been earmarked to be viciously targeted and attacked through various media channels. A campaign of character assassination was mounted and led to his eventual resignation from the RACS position, in fear for himself and his family.

This type of asymmetric warfare was becoming a highly adopted weapon of choice at the time. I had already experienced the impact of social media vilification, however, this was nothing in comparison to what lay ahead.

Mona Shindy

Chapter 3:
Hijab (September 2014 onwards)

For years, the hijab has been identified by those in the western world – which is my world – as synonymous with the subjugation and devaluing of women. It conjures up ideas of male domination, patriarchy and female disadvantage and repression.

For me, it is both easy and difficult to comprehend how this basic piece of material could elicit such negative reactions and judgement.

The judgement is easy to understand because, in some cultures where the hijab is worn, women are genuinely degraded and devalued by men. It is no secret that a significant proportion of men in some predominantly Islamic nations choose to conflate old cultural practices and beliefs that limit and disadvantage women with the correct practice of Islam.

On the flip side, it is also difficult to understand the implied negativity when one knows the purpose of the hijab is to honour and respect a way of life concerned with worshipping the creator. It is a quandary for many but, in the circles I move in, most women who wear a hijab are strong, educated, independent, liberated and highly assertive.

Despite my awareness, finally summoning the courage to wear a hijab in public was incredibly difficult for me. It wasn't because I had no familiarity with the hijab or how it physically felt to have my head covered. I had worn the hijab almost every day of my life since my teenage years but always in private and only when engaged in daily prayers. My mother wore a hijab as a standard part of daily attire, as did most of my sisters-in-law who either worked within an Islamic community context or were full-time home and family managers.

The context I struggled with was simple. I was an Australian Navy Captain! My environment was very different to that where hijabs were regularly seen and normalised. I knew, without any doubt, the hijab would bring unwanted attention, judgement and questions.

Nobody wilfully seeks to deal with more trouble than is absolutely necessary. As humans, we are constantly looking for the paths of least resistance, increased levels of comfort, efficiency and belonging. We are tribal in our behaviours, learning and responding to social cues in order to get on and get ahead. It is for all these reasons that donning a hijab in a predominantly non-receptive and subconsciously biased community does not make a lot of sense to most level-headed people and, as a highly pragmatic individual myself, these realities were at the foundation of my previous decisions not to wear a hijab in public.

It was my mother, however, who first talked me out of it when I was eighteen.

Delighted to be done with the routine of school, I'd embarked on university life, excited to be challenged and inspired by the liberal education, debating and critical thinking opportunities before me.

One day, I returned home in a heightened state after clearly winning an argument about the irrefutable existence of God. "I'm ready," I announced to my mother as I walked in the door. "I'm ready to embrace everything it means to be a proud Muslim woman. I'm going to start wearing the hijab."

My mother, a wise and much more experienced lady than I was, sat me down for what was a very heavy and frank counselling session. She was worried for me.

"Women who wear the hijab are subject to abuse and disrespect. These ladies endure hurtful putdowns or are just dismissed and ignored because of the hijab. There was also that time a man tugged on Aunty Asma's veil, making her lose her balance. She was nearly run over by a bus!" she explained, drawing on stories from her own life experiences.

She reminded me I was already a very devout Muslim living a good life, well-aligned with God's expectations. "The small extra step of a hijab will not add significantly to your standing with the creator, nor will its absence be a deal-breaker for your spiritual success on the day of judgement," she advised, almost pleading for me to have a change of heart.

"Hang on a second, Mum," I protested. "The Quran and Sunna are pretty clear on dress codes for both men and women."

"You are still young and haven't even started your working life. People will disadvantage you because of the hijab. There are even verses in the Quran and stories in Hadith that excuse normal obligations in the face of personal danger." She was passionate.

In short, my mother's position was that it was unnecessarily dangerous for me to wear a hijab publicly in Australia. Rather than define who I was, it would limit my employment and career opportunities and ultimately stop me from achieving my full potential.

Yes, it was somewhat ironic of her to give me this advice while she herself chose to wear the hijab. This observation was not lost on me, but I trusted my mother implicitly as her guidance was always well-anchored in evidence and logic. Almost without question, I put her advice into practice.

Interestingly, as a testament to her superior persuasion skills, I failed to convince my own daughter not to wear the hijab some twenty-seven years later, despite using exactly the same reasoning my mother used on me. It could have had something to do with the delivery, but it was more likely due to the changing times that have made our young adults increasingly fiercely independent from their parents. In other words, they simply don't listen!

It is telling how many Muslims understand the risks associated with visibly identifying as being of Islamic faith within Australian society and organisations. There remains a strong feeling in the community that, although acceptance is purported, the underlying truth is that visible adherence to Islamic practice is not welcome.

"I don't have any issues with Muslims, but do you really have to wear a hijab?"

"Do you really have to fast?"

"Do you really have to pray?"

Even my brother, Mohamed, made the effort to ring me directly to discuss nothing else other than my decision to wear a hijab publically.

"I don't think it is a good idea, Mona. You'll get burnt". He wanted to protect me. This comment, coming from one of the most committed Muslims I know, goes some way to explaining just how fearful Muslims were and still are to this day.

And so it was, after considerable inner debate of the pros and cons, that I started wearing the hijab publicly in 2014. I was forty-five. It may be thought that this was late in life, after my prime, especially when you consider that the hijab is essentially about the preservation of modesty. However, it is so much more than a veil that protects from the unwanted gaze; it is a symbol of identity, a constant reminder of a person's sworn conviction and an important anchor on which communities associate, build and create bonds of belonging.

While the hijab has been given negative connotations in some parts of the world, for Muslims it carries immensely positive meanings. It speaks of the values carried by those who wear it and honours women and their contributions to the community; highlighting them as entitled to respect and protection.

For me, the hijab is also very much about legacy and how my children and hopefully, one day, their children, remember me. It is important to me that I live a life that helps enrich, inform and protect the wellbeing of those who follow.

Living by full example is powerful.

My first official day wearing the hijab under the gaze of the public was when I was on my way with my husband and son to board a flight to Saudi Arabia to attend *Hajj*, the Muslim pilgrimage.

The pilgrimage is a once-in-a-lifetime obligation for all Muslims who have the financial means and physical ability to participate. For many, it signifies an opportunity for renewal; a fresh start after a clearing of the slate and the seeking of redemption for any past lapses. As part of my personal pilgrimage, I was determined to live all aspects of my faith tradition, including the wearing of the hijab, from that point on.

Receiving a full-body X-ray on my way through security, I noticed my husband and son being led away. As I watched, they became engaged in what appeared to be an intense conversation with a Border Force official. He had them against the wall and, as they later informed me, was interrogating them about where they were going and for what purpose.

Mona Shindy

"Where's the money?" the officer demanded.

"What money? We aren't carrying any," Mohamed explained.

"How are you going overseas without any money?" the officer asked.

"We are on a pre-paid tour with a group of others to attend the holy pilgrimage in Mecca," my son explained. "We'll use our credit cards, as we always do overseas if we need to buy anything."

"Is that the only place you are going? Are you crossing over any borders? Any other countries?"

Mohamed said the suspicion in the officer's voice was palpable.

This had never happened to us before and I was convinced that my hijab was what led us to be singled out for special treatment. We had been profiled.

I felt small and disrespected. We were upright, hardworking and engaged citizens, contributing to the betterment of the nation and the safety of its people in every way and at every opportunity we could. The whole incident was outrageous.

"They're now treating us like criminals with something to answer for," I said to Mohamed as we made our way to the gate. I could see he was fuming.

I looked at my son. He was seventeen – excited to be heading overseas having just finished a challenging Year 11 school year. His whole life was ahead of him to look forward to and yet, here he was being interrogated and harassed; told through actions that he was different to other Australians.

There are those who might argue that the Officer was just doing his job. There were, after all, a handful of radicalised individuals who had made their way to battlefields in Syria through Turkey. What did that have to do with us, though? Why was my beautiful, kind-hearted, happy-go-lucky son being shoved into a repugnant box by his own nation?

These are the kinds of incidents that deeply scar individuals and their families. They alienate and divide. They are discriminatory and wrong. What should have just been an uneventful and physically uncomfortable flight to Singapore, became a little more painful for me; not due to any extra cramped seating but due to what had become a lifelong emotional burden of consoling my child and rebuilding his damaged confidence.

Before heading off overseas for the pilgrimage, I had taken my executive team aside. "Guys, I know you will all do a top job holding the fort while I'm gone. I also just want to let you know that I have decided to wear the hijab after I get back from the pilgrimage. The pilgrimage is a really important life milestone for me and I hope to embrace everything it means to be a fully practising Muslim from this point on in my life. I'm just preparing you all so no one is surprised," I advised while smiling in the most casual way possible.

The conference room was quiet for a few awkward moments. Some in the team reciprocated with warm smiles. It felt like they were already very surprised and didn't know how to respond.

"Well, I hope you have a great trip. I wish you safe travels," my commercial manager said. This instantly broke the ice and the others present chimed in with similar comments as the meeting dispersed.

"Good luck."

"Have fun."

"Stay safe."

Despite their knowledge of my decision, nothing prepared me for the reactions of surprise I had from many in my organisation when they first noticed my new look.

There were literally those who could no longer make eye contact. Others kept running back and forth past my office, trying to get a glimpse of my clothing. Word had spread through the organisation like a wildfire. It was quite difficult for many, including myself. The visible cognitive dissonance generated by a simple piece of cloth was palpable.

I felt very uncomfortable. I was now the subject of debate and gossip in my organisation; like a new controversial exhibit in a museum needing to be understood. I was being gawked at and analysed. I was the subject of secret conversations that would instantly stop when I was within earshot.

"She's lost it."

"Why would you wear something restrictive like that?"

"She looks weird."

"Good on her, I say. I respect her choice."

These were just the comments I did manage to pick up in passing or while I was coincidentally hidden from view when standing behind the communal kitchenette.

Finding strength through a determination to finally live all of my truth and embrace all that I value, I found myself calling my team together again – this time to communicate why things were changing for me personally and answer any questions they had. It has always been important to me that people remain true to themselves, without fear of discrimination; to be respected for their varying views and contributions. For me, cohesive, inclusive and respectful work and social frameworks allow people to give their best and be at their best.

On that first day back in the office, I was more ready than ever to be the change I wanted to see in the world. I was happy to lead by example, to give people permission to do the same and help others understand why it was important.

I remember sitting as a solitary figure at the front of a large conference room packed with all my staff. Strangely, I felt incredibly vulnerable and alone. It wasn't the loneliness leaders feel due to the responsibility and accountability they carry at the top of an organisation; it had a whole lot to do with now being noticeably different to the majority. I knew I was respected by my team and, at the end of what had been a highly successful three-year posting, where the organisation was profoundly and positively transformed by the work we had done together, I felt they trusted me enough to openly speak their minds.

Finally, they had permission to sit and freely examine what I was wearing. I showed a video I had put together and regularly presented to ship crews before they were deployed to areas with high Muslim populations. It was designed to inform and educate on the important aspects of Islamic cultural practice. The room was silent as people absorbed what they'd seen and reflected on what was before them. There were some kind smiles, which brought me comfort, but it would be fair to say many looked stunned. I opened the floor up for questions and received a few; more politely offered to ease the awkwardness of the situation rather than to seek knowledge or clarify any information presented. I appreciated those kind gestures very much.

"Has the work now been done to include the hijab as a dress option in Navy uniform policy?" someone asked so as to acknowledge the importance of making structural changes in support of workplace diversity and inclusion.

"Are there halal meals on the ships now?" was another question posed.

Job done, ice broken, I dismissed the gathering and went back to my office for a strong coffee and some quiet reflection. A couple of hours later, one of my young lieutenants was at the door. He asked if he could talk to me, and I offered him a seat at the small round table, away from my cluttered desk.

"I wanted to thank you for getting us all together as you did just before. We have been talking about you and what you said all afternoon," he declared.

"Really? Nice things only, I hope?" I was impressed by his maturity and candour.

"We need more people like you," he continued. "I admire your courage. It's so important to our Navy and to our nation that people are able to freely speak their truth. Live their truth." He added that he felt sure my life decisions would profoundly change our Navy and society for the better.

It was an incredibly lovely gesture from this young man and it made me feel very happy. For me, it re-affirmed the value and power of open, authentic and compassionate two-way conversation between people.

I thanked him, then couldn't help myself: "Good to know you spent a whole afternoon gas-bagging with the boys," I teased. "Did you get any work done?" This is what I loved about my team – the camaraderie, the ability to be open and honest and to have a laugh.

Shattering Identity Bias

The young man stood up with a huge smile on his face and made his way to the door. At the last minute, he turned and gave me one final piece of information. "By the way Ma'am, you have your rank insignia on backwards," he said with a good dose of cheekiness and well-deserved comeback. "Just thought you should know."

After he left, I looked down at my shoulders. To my horror, I saw I was, as he'd pointed out, astern. The long time away from the office, walking the desert in Saudi Arabia, had not only given me a fantastic tan but also resulted in some sloppy attention to detail as I rushed to get dressed that morning. The worry about wearing the hijab for the first time at work probably also had a fair bit to do with it!

Mona Shindy

Chapter 4:
Media

Against the backdrop of intense daily media coverage and an unrelenting government narrative relating to an imminent Islamist terrorist threat, an Australian Navy Captain presenting as a devout Muslim in a hijab was certainly going to be an incredible interest story. Furthermore, it was a story Navy could effectively use to get its desired messaging out about being progressively ahead of the curve in relation to 'diversity and inclusion', cultural reform thinking and initiatives.

In the words of the Chief of Navy's strategic communications adviser of the time: "We are always looking for good material to get the word out about Navy activities and to present a positive image. It is hard to get traction though, and something like 'the hijab with uniform' will certainly get noticed." The hijab, it seemed, presented itself as an opportunity for Navy to 'exploit'.

The media interest was almost instantly feverish. I was increasingly seen as a 'commodity' by news reporters eager to secure interviews with me and other Defence leaders. The idea of a Navy Captain in a hijab was apparently perfect for gaining attention; attention that could then be leveraged by some for the generation of media revenue. Other organisations, with their many different motivations, also saw my story as something that could be manipulated to progress their own agendas.

There were some who analysed my engagement with media as a sell-out for the celebrity status, although it was never about that for me. Of course, I wanted to do a great job for Navy – it was about doing something positive to build Navy capability – but I would be lying if I said I did not see any altruistic secondary opportunities that could flow from the attention and interest. I looked upon the media interest as an opportunity to make a difference for my family and the broader Australian Muslim community, particularly the youngsters. I took my role seriously and spoke frankly and openly about many issues contributing to and affecting Islamic culture. I considered this essential to recognising some of the barriers impacting greater integration and understanding.

By dictionary definition, the word 'culture' means 'the ideas, customs and social behaviour of a particular people or society'. As with any other culture, Islamic community culture is affected by changing environments. Although the tenets and principles of religious beliefs never change, a society's interaction with the world is very much adjusted by analysis of the stimulus around it, and I was communicating many traditional and modern ideas not usually given prominent air time or circulation.

This information didn't seem to matter when relayed in well-researched though obscure academic papers, but I soon became aware that it was somehow unpalatable when communicated by an Australian Muslim. I'd been the subject of social media trolling before but I could see things were quickly becoming 'next level'. There were some who were determined to frame and discredit.

Some observers soon became very threatened and unhappy about me providing information from a Muslim person's perspective and understanding. Commentary around a paper I had given to the Royal United Services Institute – titled *Islam in Australia 2015: an Australian Muslim Perspective* – gave a clear insight into what some people believed should be the permissible limits regarding the views Muslims are free to express.

Former army officers and counter-terrorism experts say the navy's most senior Muslim officer crossed the line when she published her political views through an official Twitter account. But they are at odds over whether she should be allowed to Tweet again. (The Australian 2016)

The problem I had was that my communication of Muslim sensitivities, a key objective of the Islamic Cultural Adviser appointment, was argued by some to be political commentary.

A perception had been developed that I was utilising a quick-growing platform to somehow balance what had become a prominent and intensely negative national narrative about Muslims in general and, it seems, this perception was not only the cause of some discomfort but apparently was due cause for a round of name-calling.

> *Muslimus-chickus Australis*
>
> *A phone call from Keysar Trad at the Islamic Friendship Association today requesting clarification of my last post. The use of the word "mole", describing Mona Shindy was misleading, he tells me, because the word "mole" has at least five different meanings attributed to it.*
>
> *So what did I mean by calling her a mole?*
>
> *According to my copy of the 14th century Islamic scholar and jurist Shihabuddin Abu al-'Abbas Ahmad ibn an-Naqib al-Misri's masterpiece, 'The Reliance of the Traveller'', the possible meanings for "mole" are:*
>
> *(a) A spy (b) A dark skin blemish (c) A small burrowing animal with dark velvety fur (d) (Australian & NZ slang) A woman of loose sexual morals. A bitch, a slut or a prostitute who likes to sleep around a lot. A gal who likes to hang out with all the officers and enlisted men (depending on how many drinks she's had at the time) and engages in all sorts of rumpy-pumpy, sits on their knees and loudly sings bawdy sailor songs through a drunken haze all night (but not*

> *during Ramadan), and generally looks to getting laid as often as possible so that she can pretend to be a genuinely awesome Aussie chick while she's secretly engaged in a treacherous campaign to Islamicize the ADF. (e) (Arcane) A wonderful woman from Australia's Muslim community.**
>
> *Of course, I tell Trad, I meant (e).*
>
> ** From the Latin "Wonderfulis muslimis-chickus ex-communitas Australis." (Commonly abbreviated by both Tacitus and Marcus Aurelius to "mole.")*
>
> ("A Clarification" 2016)

Disagreeing with and decrying my opinions was one thing but when the vilification turned personal, that was something else entirely.

To top everything off, there was a growing unease within Defence and its retired community around the artificially amplified focus Navy was seemingly giving to what some labelled 'politically correct tokenism'.

With a clear mandate to educate on Islamic cultural issues and increase understanding within Navy, I was constantly being drawn into discussions about a Muslim's compatibility with the Australian Defence Force and, more broadly, Australia's national interests. There was scepticism from many quarters about my personal motivations or those of anyone who claimed any association with the religion of Islam. At times, I felt pressured into justifying myself.

Right-wing commentators loved creating a conspiracy narrative. They were skilled in whipping up fear and division and stoking the fire of what had become normalised anti-Muslim dog-whistle politics under the Abbott Liberal Government. For all the talking these groups do about protecting 'free speech', it seems the only valid and permissible perspectives are their own.

There were also elements within the retired Defence community that characterised my presence as a threat.

"She's degrading the sanctity of revered traditions of honour and respect built over years in the military," one retiree announced.

Apparently, I was a distraction from the real and important business of building Defence capability and defending the nation and its high-priority interests. Retired servicemen challenged me many times: "What is this need to wear hijab with your uniform?" It was as though I had desecrated the uniform. "It's called a uniform for good reason!"

There were even members of the Australian Muslim community who were not convinced by my message of inclusion and opportunity for their children within Navy, especially given the prevailing negative national narrative about Muslims and scepticism about Australia's national interests in foreign war zones. Understandable because many in the community had distant families who were suffering.

"She doesn't represent us. She is not a real Muslim" were comments made by a self-proclaimed religious leader when he discovered I was being invited to speak at a Muslim community event. The associated commentary against his social media posts also gave good insights into the many disagreements and conflicts that occurred within the Muslim community as to who should or could speak and represent the whole. The controversy he whipped up was enough to have the event organisers remove me from the line-up of speakers. They didn't want to manage the risks, even if they didn't agree with the objector.

It was a time of intense media hostility and the Muslim community was ill-prepared to respond in either a coherent or united way. Everyday Muslims, many with only a rudimentary understanding of their religion, were being approached and expected to provide deep theological responses explaining various aspects of Islamic teachings.

Mona Shindy

"What is Jihad?" was a common question.

Whether it was everyday Muslim citizens who gave clumsy and inaccurate responses to questions, or Imams and Sheiks who struggled to provide clear explanations in broken English, the Muslim identity, particularly that of Muslim women, was often co-opted and negatively manipulated by the media and other groups with ulterior motives or fears.

Despite these situations – including the pushback, judgements and vilification – causing frustration and angst, both personally and professionally, the truth is that most people I came across, both inside and outside Defence, were incredibly supportive and eager to celebrate both myself and the cultural reforms Navy was making. Difficult and challenging issues are often the first that come to mind and most strongly colour our memories of a given time or situation – this is human nature and, at the very least, certainly how my mind works as an engineer trained in critical thinking. While it is important to acknowledge and learn from the negatives, the positives are equally, if not more, important.

I would be lying if I said gaining acceptance as a cultural minority is easy or that there is a proven formula that can be used. Unfortunately, I can attest that being able to speak personal truths and be true to oneself without it becoming an issue for others remains a challenge that still needs effort and attention within some areas of Australian society.

Chapter 5:
Not my Navy – Reputation at All Costs

In 2015, I was posted to Canberra. At the time, my children were all well-settled and in important years at school and university and Mohamed was also in a good job he was happy to be doing. I considered it unreasonable to expect the whole family to relocate with me – particularly Mohamed, given he had dedicated so many years solely to the care of the family and the home, both in Australia and during my posting to the US as Liaison Officer. I made the decision to leave the family in Sydney and commute back and forth from Canberra each week. This separation added to what was quickly shaping up to be a very challenging year.

For the first time in my career, I was exposed to the Canberra environment, its decision-making committees and interfaces with the government. It was a difficult situation to be parachuted into as a Navy Captain in charge of a complex acquisition program, especially given I'd had no previous experience or training in capability development and very little knowledge of how Defence governance worked away from the waterfront. The posting also coincided with the One Defence reform program and the landscape was changing rapidly.

After my cultural reform work and the struggles of the previous years, 2015 saw me recognised and honoured through a number of national awards that acknowledged my career achievements and contributions to date. I had successfully led many complex projects and initiatives for Defence in some particularly difficult and arduous conditions. I always pursued my appointments and taskings with great dedication and enthusiasm. I loved making things happen and through the process continued to develop my own leadership style and approach. I invested much of myself into what I did professionally, leveraging a unique authenticity built on personal values. I cared deeply about those I worked with, drawing much satisfaction from supporting their individual triumphs against broader organisational imperatives. It started with the award of a Conspicuous Service Cross through the Australia Day Honours List for my contributions as Navy's Strategic Islamic Cultural Adviser. I was then named runner-up 2015 NSW Woman of the year. To top the year off, in November, at a very lavish gala dinner in Melbourne, I was announced as the 2015 National Telstra Business Woman of the Year for my achievements as an engineering executive, program manager, change agent and organisational director.

This award was an absolute highlight for me and a lovely acknowledgement of all my effort and sacrifices. The Telstra Business Woman of the Year awards are the longest-running award program for women in Australia and recognise the achievements of women from a wide range of industries who challenge the 'norms' in their fields.

The ambassador of the awards and Chief Operations Officer, Kate McKenzie, spoke of all the winners' resolve and determination that year, saying we'd all "pushed the boundaries and truly innovated in [our] respective categories".

When interviewed, I attributed my success to my values of collaboration, inclusion and empowerment. "As a senior military officer and engineer, project director and business leader, being successful as a female has always just been one piece of the puzzle."

It was all very humbling and I felt incredibly privileged to be Australian. I was extremely grateful for all the kind words of support and encouragement that I heard from many different people throughout the year. It was an experience that was very different from many previous ones that had made me feel my position as an Australian who belonged was somehow tenuous. These acknowledgements evoked emotions in me that were in sharp contrast to others I had previously felt when my right to call myself Australian had been undermined, challenged and questioned. Years of dedicated service, contribution and sacrifice wearing the Australian Navy uniform were now being celebrated – very publicly, loudly and broadly. I was seen, appreciated and rewarded as a true and deserving Australian.

On the surface, it would have appeared that I was cruising, but all the extra attention, not only from the awards but also from the rapid growth of my public profile through invitations to speak at gatherings and on media platforms, soon created increased pressures for me. Navy had encouraged wide engagement from diverse audiences – television, newspapers, magazines, radio, conferences, school assemblies and community events. I spoke at many different gatherings and settings, engaging diverse audiences. With more coverage, positive reactions contributed to the momentum for change – but also saw a growing undercurrent of negativity and fear.

The demands on my time increased markedly with organisations looking to collaborate, media seeking to cover an interest story, and the Muslim community who were, in the main, keen to engage with me as a role model for the community.

The weekly commute between Sydney and Canberra had disrupted my ability to maintain a healthy routine and balance. I was on a steep learning curve under pressure to deliver capability business cases to the government in my rapidly developing and changing work environment. However, my work ethic – forward-leaning, responsive and can-do – remained stable, despite these mounting pressures. I have this tendency to just crank things up a gear and to find ways of meeting all expectations, and although I was both physically and emotionally exhausted towards the end of 2015, I continued to say yes to too many things.

I knew I was overloaded and was frustrated I couldn't dedicate the required time to all aspects of my life that year – particularly my family. It was a strange situation to be in; one that required a strict prioritisation of time and activities but also one that presented wonderful opportunities through the establishment and rapid growth of a platform for sharing diverse perspectives. I was determined to do the best I could for everyone who now seemed to want to have a piece of me – my Navy employer, women's advocacy and business groups and the Muslim community.

With more intensity than I can ever remember, the year had also been characterised by the demonisation and politicisation of the Islamic faith. The backdrop of the Islamist ISIS international threat and an almost singular focus on border security by the Government at the time had created a hostile environment for Australian Muslims. For a practising Muslim, it often felt as though the basic human right pertaining to freedom of religion was constantly threatened. Many in the community, including myself, were being asked to answer for the behaviours of a small minority of criminals who claimed an association with the faith. Our clothing was mocked in parliament, our loyalty to the nation was questioned, our faith gatherings were hijacked as opportunities for politicians to denounce terrorism and Muslim leaders to show agreement while promising to do more, the interpretation of our scripture was manipulated and our kids were singled out for special de-radicalisation education and monitoring.

Along with the tense social and cultural climate came online trolling, which had been happening for some time but was now becoming increasingly ugly and confronting. No longer comfortable with the visceral impact it was having on me, and inexperienced with how to best deal with trolling, I soon sought assistance from the Navy Communication and Coordination Team. I wanted help to address the negative harassment and defamation of which I was now a clear target.

The @NavyIslamic Twitter handle was set up for me as an 'official' Defence social media account. Navy's communications subject matter experts recommended the social media approach as a reasonable way to counter or, as they put it, "drown out the ill-informed and offensive commentary with positive news stories, facts and educative material". They advised it was impractical to remove anything offensive from websites over which the Defence organisation had no control.

With limited training, no social media experience and minimal awareness of the risks at play, I began my adventure on Twitter with what I now know to be the highly gullible objective detailed in my original post: *Talk, share, learn # my first tweet*.

Following the advice given me by the Navy Communications Subject Matter Experts (SMEs), I tweeted about everything and anything on the @NavyIslamic handle. I set about aiming to educate as per my mandate and to demonstrate the relatability and similarity of the lives of Muslim Australians to that of the majority. I posted tweets related to my work, my career, my family and to Islamic cultural practices and sensitivities. "As long as it is factual, it will be alright," I was told. When the Twitter handle was marked as 'official' and I was profiled in uniform on the title bar, the Navy Communications Team were careful to include a disclaimer that read: "Following/Re-Tweeting does not equal endorsement."

It was following a period of calm, where I felt this platform was having the intended effect, that the rumblings started. This Twitter handle, set up to solve the trolling issues, became an avenue for detractors to generate controversy and derail cultural reform progress in relation to Islamic inclusion. There were persistent accusations that my attempts to communicate sensitivities around issues affecting Islamic community ideas were political and that I had breached a key requirement for Defence, as an instrument of government, to remain apolitical.

I was being ruthlessly discredited. Content was not the issue, but who was saying it! What upset me most about the Twitter controversy and the associated online and mainstream media pile-on is that no one had alerted me to anything they considered inappropriate or 'crossing a line' from a political perspective. Navy SMEs monitoring the Twitter handle had raised no concerns, presumably because they did not notice any. The senior officers within Defence and the Minister of Defence, who were also following the Twitter handle, had not raised concerns. The support I thought I had was not effective when I most needed it.

I was, however, most disgusted by the lack of decency shown by the detractors who ultimately decided to blindside me and the Defence hierarchy by creating controversy through plentiful approaches directly to politicians, anti-Muslim lobby groups and right-wing media commentators. That, of course, speaks to the motives. It was clear to me that those who dug up and referenced obscure Defence instructions on 'public comment' pre-dating anything to do with social media, those who had politicised almost everything to do with my religious identity, and those who sought to destroy were not concerned about Defence policy; they were out to curtail and derail the 'Islamic cultural adviser' initiative. They were malicious, vicious and merciless when it came to character assassination and defamation. It was akin to psychological warfare.

A range of attack strategies employed by groups and individuals were energised through coordinated messaging in like-minded online communities. From highly offensive blogs and anonymous threatening letters sent to my work address, to emails sent to myself and the Defence hierarchy protesting the introduction of the hijab with uniform and questioning the fitness of Muslims to serve and hold a security clearance, the onslaught was relentless. On change.org, there was even a petition circulating through the receptive online echo chambers, calling for my sacking.

After what had been a largely productive and positive year, worthy of celebration, this onslaught, which I can only describe as a well-orchestrated ambush and social media blindsiding, started in early December and intensified across the Christmas New Year period with mainstream right-wing media joining the chorus when I, and most of Defence's senior leadership, were on leave.

Initially, I reported the negative commentary to the Chief of Navy's office via his Chief of Staff and sought assistance from the Navy Communication and Coordination Team to block offensive protest emails. I also desperately wanted support from my employer to address the online vitriol, vilification and defamation as well as to identify and seek prosecution of those who had threatened me via direct mail. I naturally assumed my Navy tribe – my leaders, my teammates and my colleagues – would come to my assistance and defence.

How wrong can one person be?

The Chief of Navy's reaction and his response was, at best, muted. For too long, it was non-existent. It felt like the hierarchy was in panic mode and I soon realised my activities were being scrutinised by colleagues tasked by the Chief of Navy to work out how the controversy had started and to determine where the fault lay. Not once in the heat of the frenzy did I receive a phone call from the Chief to inquire how I was doing or to ask me for more information on my response to the claims being levelled against me and the Navy organisation. The singular focus seemed to be on organisational damage control.

I wondered whether the Chief of Navy was angry, as he was also now in the firing line. I also wondered if, without all the facts, confirmatory bias played into the decisions he made at the time. Being totally excluded from Defence's response to the crisis, it is impossible to feel any other way. It seemed to me that a view that I had breached policy in relation to making 'political comment' was formed quickly from advice given by the external detractors. From the information I gained via Freedom of Information (FOI), I know that some of those communicating outrage were previous military personnel who were now accusing the Chief of having poor judgement for even entertaining an Islamic cultural advisor role. Of course, it was the previous Chief who had established the role and set the guidelines for its objectives, not the current Chief of Navy who had inherited this initiative and, more specifically, a directly-reporting strategic cultural adviser. The whole program, of which he'd had no control in establishing, was now under fire.

Another negative consequence of how I was treated at the time and how the Defence response was observed, was eloquently described to me by several influential and mainstream Australian Muslim women who all wondered about what it meant for the broader community.

"If someone who has sacrificed so much, worn the military uniform and protected the nation against threats for decades can so easily have their intentions, status and belonging questioned, then what hope do regular, everyday Muslim citizens, just trying to get on with life, have?" Many were questioning whether there was any point in continuing to contribute to consultations relating to policy formulation or apparent efforts to learn and unite.

It felt like the inroads made to build bridges and strengthen Australian society and the ADF were all significantly damaged in such a short space of time.

I have never fully recovered from how I was managed after the social media controversy of 2015. I still have flashbacks of the Chief of Navy's expression and words when I later spoke with him about his plans for my future postings and the issues I'd faced.

For a long time, I was furious. I had taken on the role of Navy's Strategic Adviser on Islamic Cultural Affairs in good faith. I truly believed that Navy and its senior leaders had resolved to live by their espoused diversity narrative.

What I discovered, though, was that nothing had truly changed. Symbolic gestures were all the organisation could tolerate at the time. When I most needed to feel included and protected by my tribe, I felt judged and managed at arm's length.

Hindsight is a valuable thing – though entirely useless at the point it occurs.

It was inevitable that the Islamic cultural adviser role would create public discourse about Islam and women serving in the Defence Forces. Indeed, that was one of the fundamental purposes of the position. It was also inevitable that I, along with Navy, would likely become the subject of ignorant, ill-informed narrative or other criticism in the course of public debates raising what, for some people, might seem to be difficult and confronting issues about Islam, women and serving in the Australian Navy.

What was unexpected was the level to which the fallout rose.

I know Defence leadership was aware of the uncertainty many felt about the utility and need for the Islamic cultural adviser role because the FOI documents I secured also revealed that, besides actors from Defence's retired community, some serving senior officers also had reservations about the progressive inclusion and diversity initiatives being pursued that related to Muslims and other minorities. These initiatives were seen by some as overkill. The work Defence was now doing to accommodate the needs of diverse groups was argued to be disproportionate and unreasonable given their small numbers within the greater Australian demographic. Such work was seen as an unnecessary distraction that took resources away from the real 'war-fighting business' of Defence.

In other words, these people argued Defence was incapable of walking and chewing gum at the same time. Besides the resource issue, which was insignificant given work such as this was generally done as a collateral duty, another argument that such initiatives 'engendered division within the ranks' gave a clearer insight into the sentiments and motivations that drove the resistance. No doubt, these were the same arguments being proffered when women were first integrated at sea in the 1980s. Things were changing and the old guard wasn't happy.

Yet, all it was at that stage was a rumbling in a number of echo chambers about 'Defence leadership having lost their way'.

"Many just kept their unease quiet," I was later told by the Chief of Navy. "They were reluctant to voice their concerns to the previous Chief who had initiated and championed the program."

Such is the power and nature of an institution where the Chief of Navy can decide the future of any subordinate at his 'complete pleasure'. So, instead, the dissatisfaction was murmured in private and permeated out to like-minded interest and lobby groups who would ultimately engage with politicians and media to launch a personal attack on me and an attack on the Defence leadership who were seen as responsible for driving the diversity and inclusion initiatives.

For me, the personal toll of the ongoing controversy was profound. However, it wasn't the media criticism that hurt me the most but the way Navy senior leadership chose to deal with the situation. Panic mode is the only way I can describe what it felt like to me. It seemed that they were desperate to make the aggressive allegations go away as expediently as possible.

For me, it felt like a military force in retreat.

Unfortunately, Navy was ill-prepared and ill-equipped to deal with the onslaught of public criticism around Defence management and governance processes. The view they formed was quick and without consultation with me. My needs and interests were deprioritised in favour of the reputation of the organisation and senior officers. I felt as though I was disposable. As had other Muslim women before me, I felt I was again paying the price to be sacrificed during a public discussion about very important issues. When real contributions from people like me were the nation's best chance at creating meaningful protections and social resilience, I was not supported or protected strongly enough. The grief I felt was devastating.

In the process of trying to quickly neutralise the scrutiny and controversy, Navy released information about me into the public domain. I was given no opportunity to comment or challenge what was said. Nor was I able to correct ambiguities that, as it turns out, were later manipulated to cause damage to my reputation.

Given that established processes required my consultation, I felt I was denied procedural fairness. I felt marginalised, ostracised, scapegoated and devalued. My organisation had set on a path of decision-making that compromised my trust. When I later raised my concerns about my management with the Chief of Navy, he explained his ultimate responsibility was as the "Steward for the Navy organisation and its reputation".

Mona Shindy

Chapter 6:
The Betrayal

What I see as 'the betrayal' started with the publication of an 'On the Record' (OTR) statement from the Chief of Navy on 6 January 2016. In it, he wrote I had been 'counselled' about my use of the @NavyIslamic Twitter account. I was given no such notice, nor was I even spoken to about any perceived misconduct.

'Counselling' is, of course, a specific form of adverse administrative action available to commanders. The OTR statement conveyed to the world that I had been the subject of adverse disciplinary action. This was a matter that significantly embarrassed and undermined me and my reputation, given I had not been the subject of any such action. Again, there was an established process by which such 'counselling', if in fact intended, was to occur. The affected individual would be given a notice in writing and have the opportunity to reply, clarify information and provide evidence and explanations relating to any incident or activities being questioned.

The wording of the OTR statement went out without consultation and I was given no opportunity to point out that such a statement would be damaging to me. Subsequently, I discovered that an earlier draft of the OTR, gained through my FOI requests, had included the words 'informal counselling' but the word 'informal' had been deleted, indicating to me that this issue had been considered and that a deliberate decision had been made to permit the damaging and inaccurate imputation against me to be made.

In dealing with a completely different FOI request from a journalist probing about my apparent 'disciplining', Defence also authorised the release of other personal private information without following its own guidelines which required it to consult with me before making a decision involving the release of such information. This failure led to the release of information purposely crafted to compare me to another Defence Force officer who had previously been dismissed for repeatedly disobeying orders. It was done to address his lawyer's claims that the Defence hierarchy appeared to be implementing inconsistent discipline given I was not losing my job.

Although I can understand the hierarchy's motives and purpose for clarifying the distinction between my situation and that of the other officer; the released information again reinforced the idea that I had been administratively disciplined and that my suitability for continued service was considered. It was again released without prior notice to me, directly to a journalist which resulted in further damage to my reputation as well as significant distress when I first read and became aware of it in the public domain. If I had been consulted, I would have at least been made aware of the pending disclosure and been able to convince Defence not to post the information on the FOI disclosure log or to challenge the proposed disclosure through the Office of the Australian Information Commissioner due to breach of privacy concerns.

My basic rights had been disregarded and I became embroiled in a catch-22 situation whereby the finalisation of the release of my private information under one law, namely the FOI Act was used as justification to deny me having the matter considered for breach of privacy under the Privacy Act. Besides this debacle, it was also apparent that no one was considering any of Navy's obligations to me under the Workplace Health and Safety (WHS) Act.

From January to April 2016, The Australian newspaper ran a series of critical editorials and articles that worked together to discredit me, question my competence and integrity and place pressure on Defence hierarchy to defend the pursuit of their progressive inclusion and diversity agenda.

I was the subject of many articles in other media sources, like the piece published in The Spectator Australia on 14 April 2016 and headlining as *Walk the Plank*. Its opening sentence began by ridiculing the navy: It's sad to say but the *Royal Australian Navy is fast becoming a joke, if it isn't there already*.

It then went on to target me as the driving force behind the 'latest controversy':

The presenting problem is Captain Mona Shindy, one of very few female Islamic Naval officers, and most famously and troublingly, the Chief of Navy's important-sounding Strategic Adviser on Islamic Cultural Affairs.

In short, the article summarised all the ill-feeling I'd had directed towards me over a short time. It referred to my NSW Telstra Business Woman of the Year award as *'offensive to actual businesswomen who put capital and livelihoods on the line, but most of them are no doubt too busy running businesses to be spending a night dressed in a bow tie and dinner suit (accessorised with a hijab)'* and suggested that I'd become a *'pain in the stern'* to Navy, which only had itself to blame.

It also decried the whole initiative:

... The very existence of a Strategic Adviser on Islamic Cultural Affairs – a Grand Mufti-like authority on religion with a minuscule military presence – is troubling.

... the Navy (and the Army and Air Force) can do better in accommodating Muslims within the ranks. But to do it in such a gratuitous way was only ever going to alienate and divide defence personnel.

Mona Shindy

In addition, they accused me of using the @NavyIslamic Twitter account to *'retweet posts from genuine hate preachers'* and to *'criticise political parties, criticise former prime ministers, criticise Israel over Palestine, and to unofficially give the government's imprimatur to intolerance of free speech.'*

My name was plastered everywhere and I even made the national evening TV news bulletins. The published material was crafted to generate controversy and it invited more negative online commentary about me. The vitriol was intense and the defamation abundant. I was pursued by various media outlets seeking a response, those vehemently critical and others seeking to provide some balance and an alternate perspective. Of course, I was permitted to speak to nobody. Defence essentially chose to shut down all access. It was their tried and proven strategy of saying very little until other more engaging news stories took attention away from the current crisis.

I felt blamed and ostracised, and could see that my welfare was being prioritised well below that of protecting Navy reputation. "It is your personal responsibility to approach the police or take civil legal action to address this defamation," I was told. I was devastated. Already besieged and attacked psychologically through the spreading of mistruths, the lack of direct support was like that final nail in the coffin.

I was denied opportunities that involved public exposure or highlighted my association with the Royal Australian Navy.

"I do not endorse Mona accepting the University of NSW (UNSW) Judy Raper award as a serving Naval Officer. Mona can accept the award as a citizen member of the UNSW alumni, but not in uniform."

I was now being closely managed. My external exposure was limited, my words carefully examined and my career trajectory diverted and curtailed. It was all done under the guise of me being 'protected'.

I received sage pieces of advice from various senior officers who had influence over my naval career.

"You look *confronting* with the hijab."
"If you do any public speaking, you should not use your title as "Captain".

"It is best to keep a low profile until things blow over."

"The debate has become too polarised and both you and Navy will be further damaged with more engagement."

"We think it is best you remain posted as directing staff at the Australian Defence College where you are well placed to help the *other* foreign students."

The truth, though, was that the behaviours of the Defence hierarchy were alienating me. I was essentially silenced in such a way that denied my agency. Decisions were being made for me and about me without my consultation. Engagement with the media was prohibited for me and as such, I had no right to reply to some of the outlandish accusations being levelled against me. This went against the grain for me as someone who lives by speaking openly.

What made things worse was that my leaders were also eerily silent about the negative commentary pertaining to me, resulting in a distinct impression there was something to hide. I would have expected my leaders to have been out in front of me, very publicly and widely, strongly rebutting the personal attacks on my character. This did not occur. By default, it also gave legitimacy to the accusations that questioned my integrity. Ultimately, I felt very abandoned and scapegoated by those I had trusted and relied on as my leaders and mentors. As the only visible woman associated with the crisis, I couldn't help but feel long standing traditions take hold as I was 'left to hold the baby' now that the going had gotten tough.

Defence did, however, make some effort to respond to the attacks on its reputation and defended the implementation of diversity and inclusion initiatives by explaining their impact as significant capability enhancers. Their responses, however, never mentioned me by name. They never objected to or condemned the defamation, vilification and vitriol directed at me nor did they do anywhere near enough to indicate ongoing support for me. I was gagged and simply had to take whatever was thrown at me. I believe the homogeneity of thinking made it impossible for Defence hierarchy to truly understand the impact decisions being made would have on my psychological safety.

The silence made me feel that Defence personnel were complicit in allowing my public humiliation. Their selective release of some information and omission of other detail painted me as someone with poor judgment. I felt that I was made to be the 'fall guy' while Defence deflected from the many governance and process deficiencies that allowed the public controversy to take hold.

By April 2016, I was suffering from disrupted sleep, constantly needing to explain the situation I was in to family, friends and colleagues while dealing with significant hurt as many of my peers started to distance themselves from me.

I remember one particularly uncomfortable Last Post Ceremony I attended at the Australian War Memorial in 2017 while posted as a staff member at the Australian Defence College. The students I was accompanying on the field activity, all of similar rank to myself, started a straight line formation down one side of the Pool of Reflection in preparation for the ceremony that was about to commence. I joined the formation front line. By the time I arrived, the line was only about halfway down the length of the pool, so there was plenty of space for others to continue the formation after me. Instead, my colleagues chose to begin another file behind the frontline. Initially, this seemed strange as the view of activities would be clearer from the front row. What I found particularly saddening and embarrassing, however, was that the back file grew to the full length of the pool and not one person chose to stand near me to continue the line at the front. It felt like they were avoiding being associated with me or the possibility of being caught standing next to me in a photograph. The ceremony started and ended with me feeling very isolated and rejected as part of what would generally never be accepted as a non-symmetrical and unbalanced military formation.

Incensed by Defence's lack of action and what felt like complete disregard for my welfare and reputation, I wrote to the Chief of Navy in May. The email was long – totalling the equivalent of six pages and highlighting no less than twenty-four key points supporting my request for immediate action to correct the public record and clear my name.

Within the email, I outlined the current situation starting from the reason the Islamic cultural adviser role was established and its objectives, through to the Twitter debacle and the agenda to discredit me in the public eye. I summarised the areas in which my integrity and allegiance had been held up for scrutiny. I spoke of the impacts – to me personally, to my family and to my future career prospects.

My email went on to outline my frustration at being denied the opportunity to clear my name. It highlighted many examples of how Defence's management of the situation was adversely affecting me. It included a situation my son, who was completing the New Entry Officer's Course (NEOC) at HMAS *Creswell*, described to me. Apparently, the Ship's Warrant Officer (SWO) had used my Twitter story as an example of unethical behaviour during a Fraud and Ethics lesson in one of his classes.

In closing the email, I renewed my plea for Defence support to clear my name and help stop the public and internal ridicule that was causing me considerable distress. I wanted to be given permission to speak publicly about my experiences and be able to say that Defence was by my side.

To my disgust and disappointment, the end result of this communication was that the HMAS *Creswell* incident involving my son, was 'looked into'. As for the rest, I was to understand I was not the only party being attacked. I was not the only party affected by the fallout of initiatives put into place long before many current leaders were in a position to have any input. Later, my prior Chief of Navy told me the new Chief "felt he was burnt by activities that occurred before his tenure."

Eventually, I went to see our new Chief in person. I needed to talk with him directly about my concerns regarding being posted at rank, out of my professional discipline, at a time I may reasonably have expected to be promoted. Navy had posted me as directing staff to the Australian Defence College in 2017 after I had just completed the Defence Strategic Studies Course in 2016. Initially, it was presented by the then Deputy Chief of Navy as a short-term holding pattern until a suitable position, better aligned with my engineering and project director expertise, became available. It was not long before it became very apparent that I was expected to remain at the college for much longer. For me, it felt very much like a side-lining; out of sight and out of mind.

"You thought you were going to be promoted?" he snarled at me as I stood in front of his desk.

"Well, Sir, given my performance record over many years of service, my qualifications and experience as an engineer as we are about to embark on the biggest ever reconstitution of Navy assets through the national endeavour of continuous ship building, the fact I have just finished the senior officer command and staff course and that I have five years at rank, I would have thought I would have been a highly competitive candidate for promotion," I said.

The displeasure in his eyes and voice will live with me forever.

Chapter 7:
Challenged Loyalties

I struggled with loyalty. I didn't want to embarrass any of the Defence leaders or air any dirty laundry that might highlight deficiencies in Defence's culture or governance processes.

The inaction of superiors, friends and colleagues hurts infinitely more than any vicious rambling or untruth spread by faceless cowards hiding behind a veil of anonymity online or through unclaimed editorial opinion pieces within the print press.

Although always active in discussions and willing to inject alternate ideas and raise risks in decision-making processes, I had never questioned the final decisions made by my superiors.

This had to change.

I felt so aggrieved and unfairly treated that I could not just let things lie. I knew I had to do something. I resolved to speak truth to power and demand justice.

For me, it was as though I had been sacrificed overnight. My organisation and its leaders seemed singularly focused on reputation management. I had continued to hold the cultural advisor position as a collateral duty while completing the Defence Strategic Studies Course in 2016 and while employed as a directing staff member at the Australian Defence College in 2017. With Navy restricting my associated activities in 2016 and 2017, I soon lost interest in the role that was no longer supported by the hierarchy.

Mona Shindy

"We won't be having any future Iftar reception dinners engaging with the community" was just one of many determinations made by the Chief of Navy to avoid further controversy from detractors who considered such events to be incompatible with Defence's mandate.

I summarised my account of the situation – the lessons I'd learned and the remaining personal impact on me – in a final letter I wrote to the Chief of Navy in 2017, just prior to walking away from the role as Navy's Strategic Adviser on Islamic Cultural Affairs.

As I finish performing duties as your strategic adviser on Islamic cultural affairs, I provide this written record that captures my assessment of what achievements have been made and what residual considerations and challenges remain. I also seek to advise you on my progress in dealing with the personal emotional burden I have endured in relation to public commentary around my performance of duties as your strategic Islamic cultural adviser and as a result of organisational decisions made post the controversy that flared late 2015, early in 2016, around the now-closed @NavyIslamic Twitter handle. I provide the specifically personal information in the hope of explaining how certain decisions, events and management approaches have had negative impacts on me. I feel I have suffered what could have been avoidable psychological harm and long-term professional reputation damage. These feelings have subsequently translated into what I see as a 'trust deficit' for me with the organisation. Although I have absolutely no doubt that you and other senior leaders intended no malice towards me, and in fact worked hard to protect both myself and the organisation, management decisions made post the Twitter controversy further exacerbated and amplified my pain in the wake of the event. My strong desire is that organisational lessons can be learnt and improvements made to mitigate similar risks and harm to individuals in the future. I also hope that you will be able to assist me in finding closure to the current personal challenges I face, by progressing, and in some cases reconsidering the previously raised remedies I propose again in this letter.

I went on to outline the progress and cultural reform successes achieved over the last three-and-a-half years, including the increase in Navy's appeal amongst diverse Australians. I wrote about the enhanced reputation of the Australian Defence Forces abroad, gained as a result of the improved understanding and cooperation with allied nations stemming from a greater appreciation of the cultural sensitivities. Finally, I summarised many of the other inclusive changes made regarding uniform, prayer and dietary requirements.

I touched on the areas of enduring resistance, citing specific examples of aggressive questioning and discomfort amongst crew members and executives I had either directly witnessed or heard about. There were still members of the ADF that just simply felt uncomfortable and unhappy about having a visible Muslim among them. However, I also made sure to emphasise that people involved in such incidents were in the minority and that a good majority had '*been receptive, inclusive and supportive in line with what would be expected against our organisation's signature behaviours*'.

My position as 2015 National Telstra Business Woman of the Year had been curtailed by the events and controversy of 2016, resulting in lost opportunities for myself and the Navy. I was denied many speaking opportunities. Invitations were declined on my behalf in what I could only see was Navy's attempt to silence me. They claimed this was to protect me; however, I felt it was more damaging to my reputation than protecting of it.

At some length, I wrote about my observations regarding Navy's response to the controversy, using loaded words such as 'marginalisation', 'diversion' and 'passive non-compliance'.

In the letter's closure, I was able to list a series of requests that I had, including formal apologies, compensation and retraction of various communications made over the last year. I signed off with a very open and raw statement of my position at the time:

Mona Shindy

It is my strong desire that in digesting the contents of this letter and with a better understanding of the deep impact the events of last year have had on me, you will be able to agree to the remedies I have sought in this correspondence. I know some of what I have asked for will require that you agree to accept a slightly greater level of risk than you have been prepared to in the past and I hope the information I have provided will be helpful in assisting you with your consideration. I have also recently started seeing a psychologist to help me deal with things as I work to achieve a resolution I can comfortably live with in relation to my raised concerns. I hope you can understand that I have been hurting now for quite some time and am keen to quickly progress closure for myself to limit prolonged suffering.

My overarching aim, in this painstakingly penned letter, was to contribute to ongoing improvement in the culture and processes of Navy – an organisation I still deeply respected and valued despite my experiences of the last two years. I had, after all, served for twenty-eight years at that point and it was important for me to remember why. I also made sure to offer my thanks and gratitude for the opportunities I'd been afforded in my recent role, irrespective of the outcome because they had been worthwhile, and my personal learning had been significant and valuable. However, more than anything else, I was seeking an acknowledgement of what I'd been through as a means of being able to move forward, both professionally and personally.

In response to my letter, the Chief of Navy had his Chief of Staff, also a Navy Captain, do a 'fact finding'. He replied to my letter, nearly two months later, stating his intention to do no more. He asked me to "draw a line under the incident" and cited the risks of me continuing to pursue the matters.

Instead, he tried to organise a mediation, which I declined. I wanted change and action, not just more delay and distractions talking about things that would inevitably be swept under the carpet by those with no incentive to shift and all the power to do whatever they pleased.

For me, this fight was no longer about individuals – although I highly respected and cared deeply about my superiors – it was about the responsibility I had to help improve the 'national institution' for all Australians. I had made up my mind. I was committed to making a difference. After all, who else was I leaving that work for? It was about a life well-lived.

If I took no action, it would be something I would regret for the rest of my days.

Chapter 8:
Effecting Change - Political and Legal Involvement

With this conviction firmly in mind, I wrote to request an Inspector General of the Australian Defence Force (IGADF) Inquiry into my treatment arising from the execution of my duties as Chief of Navy's Strategic Adviser on Islamic Cultural Affairs. IGADF is a statutory office holder appointed by the Minister of Defence and is independent of the ADF chain of command. The IGADF provides a means of reviewing the performance of the ADF military justice system and over-sighting complaints made under the Redress of Grievance process. The incumbent can highlight shortfalls and make recommendations for improvement.

An independent investigation was conducted, albeit with tightly scoped terms of reference. I have always wondered how independent investigations that report to the Chief of the Defence Force and Minister of Defence can be fairly conducted. It is such a closed shop, where reputation is everything and those indoctrinated for long enough will fight to protect it in peace or war with the same tenacity that they would engage an enemy in conflict. Due to its very unique rules and laws as a 'total institution', Defence culture and governance deficiencies are very difficult to examine by anyone who has not been intimately involved within its ranks; indeed, by anyone who would not struggle with a sense of loyalty to protect organisational reputation just as I did. That said, I am satisfied that I had the strength of character to raise the important issues and provide evidence, both via interview and in writing, supported by many evidentiary artefacts, for this IGADF investigation and others I asked for in subsequent years. A good portion of what I raised over the years was not looked into or omitted from investigation and much of what was investigated was still veiled in a cloud of secrecy.

Although the outcome was not perfect or complete from my perspective, my fear and trepidation were allayed when I was blessed to have my IGADF complaint assigned to a highly nuanced and appropriately senior investigating officer – one who held the same rank as the Chief of Navy – who worked diligently to uncover truths. I would have loved to have included the findings of the investigation in this book but, somewhat ironically, to protect the privacy of several protagonists involved, Defence has issued orders making it an offence for me to do so. I was denied permission to speak or write about anything I had submitted or that came out of the IGADF office. Ultimately, it didn't matter to me because I knew the artefacts would be held in Defence archives and still available to future leaders who cared enough to look, as well as to media or other independent authorities such as the Australian National Audit Office (ANAO) or the Australian Human Rights Commission who might one day seek to commence their own research and analysis.

Finally, I had a report with a range of findings that validated the dismay I had been feeling. It came with a range of recommendations that, if enacted, would bring me some peace and offer an acceptable remedy.

However, the very serious issues around the release of my private information and subsequent breach of privacy were unaddressed in the report, which identified my concurrent approach to the Office of the Australian Information Commissioner (OAIC) as the most appropriate avenue to seek a determination on the fairness of Navy actions in relation to the management and public release of information pertaining to me.

Again, the response from Navy was to do nothing proactive with this report or its recommendations. In fact, only one recommendation was acknowledged but directed to me for action – the option of making a claim for reparation. It was an internal process and anything I might receive would be 'an act of grace' determined at the complete discretion of the Chief of Navy informing a ministerial delegate.

Downtrodden and weary after years of making my case repeatedly, I felt this response was yet another insult and abrogation of duty to me.

Simultaneously, Navy had been fighting tooth and nail to defend its actions regarding the handling of my private information with OAIC. This went on for over four years, with a toing-and-froing of arguments and counterarguments between myself and Defence's dispute resolution area, all facilitated through the OAIC.

Whether the material was released by internal actors recklessly or innocently, I can never be sure. What I do know is that its release ignored Defence guidelines and fuelled a wildfire of negative, sensational and humiliating reporting about me in all forms of media. My dispute with the organisation was very painful. It was essentially myself up against an army of Defence legal practitioners charged with protecting organisational reputation at all costs. They called black, white. They didn't respond to the hard questions and facts. They omitted relevant details and they claimed that they could read my mind without needing to ask. They played with and obscured the straightforward meaning of words. They stalled and asked for extensions of time to respond.

I was beginning to understand that no amount of logical reasoning or appeals made to the hierarchy's conscience would change how I was being managed. After many attempts to communicate my position, it was some time before I truly understood the futility of trying to bring about change from within the organisation.

The power imbalance meant I was helpless, forced to accept whatever was decided for my future.

Mona Shindy

The Deputy Chief of Navy stared at me from behind his desk. "You've stuffed up the whole Captains' posting plot!" he said.

I had felt so aggrieved at being written off and hidden away at the Australian Defence College, that I'd finally asked to be posted back to a role where I could maintain professional currency as an engineer and project director. Now, with this comment, I wondered if he'd wanted to put another officer into the position I was now being given. It was the only justification I could think of. With the expression of much frustration, I was reluctantly allowed to move from the Australian Defence College back to a role more aligned with my technical and business competencies as the Director of the Navy Materiel Seaworthiness Assurance Agency.

This new organisation was charged with establishing processes, systems and a battle rhythm of audit and inspection that would assure the seaworthiness of all Navy assets and equipment. Heading this critical function for Navy, I set on a path of designing, building and leading an organisation that would systematically ask the hard questions about adherence to technical policy, collect evidence confirming that adherence or otherwise and identify gaps in the system that posed risks to the seaworthiness of all Navy equipment.

In the three years I led the organisation, many deficiencies were uncovered and addressed. I felt very privileged and proud to have developed what quickly became a crucial capability for Navy, heavily relied on as a highly effective and respected technical assurance agency.

Along with this assurance work, I continued to question and challenge senior officers about non-adherence to established processes in relation to my personal management and the non-transparent posting and promotion selection processes affecting individuals of my rank and above. I didn't see why a defensible evidence-informed system of practice ensuring equity, adherence to policy and adequate record-keeping in support of decisions made should not exist. I also couldn't understand what all the secrecy was about.

In my imagination, I pictured the hierarchy sitting in their closed decision-making forums and openly discussing their distaste for me. They were unused to being challenged by subordinates. They didn't like it and, as such, I was no longer part of the 'in group'. It was like a school playground with the cool kids deciding on the fate of the outsiders. They knew they could do what they liked and get away with it.

Exclusion. Abuse. Bullying.

Except, this wasn't a school playground. This was a billion-dollar Defence organisation to which I had committed a very significant portion of my life! I understood that challenging the long-accepted status quo would have serious consequences for me personally but what was at stake was, and remains, so much bigger than me.

Despite, or perhaps due to, having my career derailed and being sidelined, I continued to be seen by superiors as a troublemaker. I asked lots of questions. I challenged normalised behaviours. I was determined to not only fight for justice but to understand the basis and justification for decisions around my management, exclusion from governance decision-making bodies and the limitations placed on any opportunities to act at a higher rank.

It made people uncomfortable.

It was a strange situation I'd found myself in. I was on the outer more than I'd ever been in my life. For the first time, my values and expectations did not align with those practised by the organisation

I had loved for over three decades. The pain I felt was emotional and ultimately led to me suffering a psychological injury. I struggled with anxiety.

I had a distinct feeling they were all waiting, perhaps even hoping, for my resignation. To admit defeat. Allowing them to go back to their old ways. It was certainly a much better outcome than having me accept a Command Initiated Transfer to Reserves (CITR); no wasted redundancy payments.

I knew I was bitter, but I also knew I had to continue to fight – if not for me, then for my children and others who might follow me.

It had become painfully clear that an external intervention was the only mechanism that might bring needed change. I considered available legal, political and media escalation avenues.

Scarred from my previous experiences, I decided media would be the last avenue where I would seek support as there were no guarantees in relation to how others would choose to frame my story. Instead, I started with the political approach and wrote to the Minister for Veteran Affairs, The Honourable Darren Chester, and the Minister for Women, The Honourable Marise Payne.

I received no reply from the Minister for Women.

The political response from the Minister for Veteran Affairs was non-committal. It summarised the actions I was pursuing regarding an internal Defence claim for reparation due to defective administration and noted and thanked me for my long military service. It also acknowledged as appropriate the actions the Chief of Navy had pursued with respect to my grievances.

I wasn't surprised. After all, what else was I expecting from a letter drafted for the Minister by the Defence Department? In fact, I believe that with such a highly visible controversy, the adopted approach would have already previously been cleared through the Minister of Defence at the time (now the Minister for Women).

The letter also stated that the Minister had asked the Deputy Chief of Navy to provide me with information regarding my non-selection for promotion and how the system works. I knew I should have gone to members in the 'opposition' but I again struggled with a sense of loyalty to the Defence organisation. I kept convincing myself, hoping against hope that somehow decency and obligations to me under the WHS Act would shift some of the decisions being made. I was also so scarred from the trauma I was dealing with at the time and I wasn't sure I had the strength then to fare anymore. I didn't want to spark another controversy.

My problem was that the prevailing rules meant that senior leaders were within their rights to make whatever decisions they wanted. Defence, as a 'total institution' with its own laws and practices, was not accountable under normal civilian industrial relations laws. In the words of one of my Defence legal advisors: "They will put you into a vortex."

But I objected anyway.

I submitted claims. Got the run-around. Supplied more information. Entered more evidence. Answered more questions.

I weathered rejections. Faced scorn. Was stalled again and again.

All the while, my physical and mental health deteriorated.

Five-and-a-half years.

The truth is, I had seen lots of information from many previous Deputy Chiefs that simply did not demonstrate rigour, a level playing field or fairness and equity, particularly in relation to the promotion of officers to the Senior Leadership Group.

There were no written records about criteria or reasons one person was found less competitive for promotion in comparison to another. Keeping such records would apparently 'breach senior officer privacy' and affect their willingness to 'say what they really thought' about a person or their 'fit' in future promotion board deliberations. It talked about determinations being time-sensitive, based on positions opening at any given time and the team character preferences of the superiors to which the vacant positions would report.

Such arguments made no sense to me from an equity perspective as opportunities were now being offered based on 'likability' and perceived, not necessarily evidence-informed, 'good fit'. These were also the same criteria being used to determine what 'grooming' opportunities individuals would or would not be given during their careers in preparation for future higher rank. The word 'groom' is used by Navy hierarchy to mean 'prepare' or 'position'. Simply put, if you groom someone over a number of years through facilitating courses, preparatory knowledge and experience building postings and networking opportunities; while not doing that for others, then you are reinforcing structural barriers that discriminate and disadvantage those who are not 'favourites'. The whole reasoning, lack of transparency, and non-evidence-based decision-making were rubbish in my mind, as they provided a structural impediment (through secrecy) that allowed a club culture supported by incontestable biases to thrive.

"If you are so good, Mona, why doesn't anyone want you?" were the words one Deputy Chief of Navy used as part of his response to my inquiries about the promotion system.

As I now understand, getting to this point was inevitable for me. I had struggled immensely, a product of the Defence 'system', to openly challenge the hierarchy. Although populated with highly intelligent and logical thinkers, the hierarchy had found it impossible to acknowledge and address poor behaviours and practices in the senior ranks. The leaders intuitively knew this would put into question the legitimacy of Defence's governance decisions in relation to personnel career and complaints management. It would mean that they would need to question the very processes, culture and behaviours that they personally had benefitted from. It is unnatural for people to challenge systems where there is no incentive to do so. For me, things didn't add up. There was a distinct lack of logic, evidence and adherence to the principles of transparency, equity, fairness and decency. Although I knew I had the resilience to cope with the injustice I felt and I had the skill sets to succeed and thrive in the pursuit of alternate activities post Defence, I simply could not disregard the strong responsibility I felt to improve an institution I had served and loved for a good portion of my working life.

In early 2021, the Information Commissioner finally made recommendations in relation to my complaints. They were all in my favour and an order was issued directing Defence to improve its governance processes to ensure affected individuals would be fairly consulted and have opportunities to redact and appeal the proposed release of any personal information.

This gave me some vindication but again, nothing tangible that would make life better for me.

The damage was already done.

Mona Shindy

Chapter 9:
Time's Up

◆

I received the news over the phone.

"Mona, I am sorry to advise that we are unable to offer you any positions within the Senior Leadership Group as it has been determined that others are a better fit. I have one 'requirements development' role for a new capability which I know you would just eat up," the Deputy Chief advised.

"What are the other options I have for jobs, Sir?" I inquired, searching for alternate opportunities that might better align with my interests.

"That's all I have, Mona," he said. "We have already kept you on as a Captain for a full three-year posting beyond the norm for someone in your position, where you are no longer competitive for promotion."

"So, nothing else? Nothing else I could be suitable for?" I was surprised my years of experience, degrees in engineering, commerce and arts, majors in politics and policy and recent strategic leadership training at the Centre for Defence and Strategic Studies (CDSS) within the Australian Defence College (ADC) had yielded nothing that I was the best candidate for.

"No, that's it. Nothing else," he said with firmness to the finality of his position.

I was silent for a few moments as I digested the actual meaning of what had just happened.

I was being told I had reached the end of the road.

The situation didn't stack up for a number of reasons. Only the previous week, a number of possible positions had been available – as discussed and documented with the Director of Navy Senior Officer Management (DNSOM) – yet they all appeared to have vanished. Further, as one of those senior officers, I was acutely aware we had skill shortages across a number of areas of Navy. The technical disciplines were particularly stretched, given that Navy had recently embarked on a major recapitalisation program of continuous shipbuilding. Recent government announcements relating to a long-term boost of Defence personnel numbers to better tackle emergent threats seemed at odds with the information I was now hearing.

Ordinarily, this sort of information would have been delivered in a face-to-face meeting by my career manager, the Deputy Chief of Navy, although he now had little option due to the prevailing COVID pandemic restrictions.

"Mona, are you still there?" he said, breaking the silence.

He understood I was not at all inspired by the idea of performing the role he had offered. "We have to think about career paths for everyone. We need to maintain healthy progression through-puts," he said. "The only other option I can offer you is a CITR."

There was no option, not really. Setting up an unpalatable situation with no reasonable alternative is what is called 'constructive dismissal' in the civilian world.

A Command Initiated Transfer to Reserves (CITR) is essentially a voluntary redundancy scheme whereby certain individuals are targeted for early retirement. It is designed to clear positions and billets for others to rise through the ranks; others who are seen to be better performers or, to use the words of the Navy career managers, a 'better fit' for the higher ranks.

Truth be told, it is a mechanism to squeeze people out and that's what was happening. I was being managed out.

The lack of justification or explanation regarding the process, the performance appraisals or the ratings was what grated. It was a closed club with language nuances and word choices acting as code for the in-group.

"Could I ask what it is about my character, competencies or personal traits that mean I could not perform very well in a number of the leadership roles that have recently become available in the Senior Leadership Group?" I enquired of the Head of Naval Engineering a few days later.

His response was mind-boggling. "You are suitable for those roles, Mona, but we have already put others in them and they are now full."

The system is always presented as a meritocracy and I would certainly never suggest that those selected do not have merit. Of course, they do! As do others; others who somehow don't make the grade when it comes to the seemingly arbitrary and ill-defined criteria of 'best fit'.

I was certainly not the first, nor will I be the last, to be given a CITR. Some would even argue I was among the lucky ones; not everyone gets this offer before, out of frustration, they choose to leave on their own accord. What I am saying is that my uniqueness would have made it more likely that I would not ever be selected as 'the best fit' for a Senior

Leadership Group role whose appointment was essentially voted on by the small homogeneous community to which it belonged.

"You should be happy, Mona!" That was how the Deputy Chief of Navy put it.

By this stage, I'd had enough. I took a good chunk of leave in the first half of 2021. I had lost that strong feeling of connectedness with the Defence institution that I once relished. At the time, I also no longer felt able to work for an organisation that didn't support me and didn't want me. I reluctantly took the CITR, more for my mental health than anything else.

My family, as always, were my greatest support. They listened patiently and empathetically for hours, days, months and years. They felt and shared every part of my pain. I don't know what might have happened to me if I didn't have their love and support or their stories and activities to distract me.

They also gave enough feedback for me to understand that my work was now having too much of a negative impact on my health and our family life.

On the many occasions I regularly offloaded on him, Mohamed would protest, "Mona, you just keep ruminating about the same stuff. Over and over again."

"Mum, we've heard this a million times. Enough already!" my daughter would snap as she tried to unwind after a tiring day at work.

I knew I needed to detach from what had become a toxic environment, where what seemed to me like abuse of power was an entrenched cultural phenomenon.

It had been a long road and I was tired. The decision I made came in 2021, on the back end of being harassed, bullied and discriminated against for a number of years.

My mind went back to what the then Deputy Chief of Navy told me in 2013 when he asked me if I would take on the Islamic Strategic Cultural Adviser role. I thought about how he'd said the Senior Leadership Group had fallen silent when asked about how receptive they might be to having a Muslim family move in next door to their family. In all that had transpired since, I wasn't sure anything had really changed at all. I was being told I was not considered a 'good fit' to be counted as part of what was, in the main, the same group.

My office was particularly neat and tidy in the last couple of weeks before I left. I had been gradually taking items home in boxes for some weeks, transforming what would normally have been a complete mess of creative scratchings on the whiteboard and piles of documents cluttering every corner of the room to a sterile and empty abode.

One message caught my eye on the card my team had given me at a farewell lunch they'd organised.

> *Thank you for all your support over the last three years. I will miss you. I really appreciate everything you have done to help me grow and develop. Best of luck with your next chapter.*

Another lovely message read:

> *You've been the best boss I have ever had. I don't know why I was ever frightened of you when you looked at me from above your glasses when we first met.*

I always remained consciously professional to the very end and had tried very hard to conceal my frustrations with how I was treated by certain members of my hierarchy. However, many in my team knew I was unhappy. Some formed their views through observing unacceptable behaviours directed at me first-hand, while others would have noticed my exclusion from higher opportunities afforded to my peers. Some had been inadvertently drawn into giving recounts of events associated with some formal complaints I had made.

I remember one very interesting conversation I had with a peer who came to visit me in my office before I left. I thought we would discuss some work our teams had been collaborating on.

"You came up in a discussion I was having with other officers this morning," she said. "They said some really disgusting and disrespectful things. I don't know why we are still like this. It just felt so *icky*." She looked at me, then away. "Well, I just felt like I wanted to see you and tell you I really respect you and wish you the very best for the future."

I didn't know exactly what she meant or who she might have been referring to. Truth be told, I didn't want to know, nor did I care anymore. I changed the topic straight away, redirecting the focus back to day-to-day work activities. I had been so damaged by this stage, I didn't feel I could bear any more triggers. It was, however, a particularly lovely gesture from a colleague; a gesture that gave me hope my time in the Navy did have a meaningful significance and would hopefully inform deeper discussions, better decisions and greater reforms in the future.

As I walked out the doors for the last time, I reflected on everything that had happened.

It is amazing how senior officers, accustomed to always getting their way with subordinates, can react when one of the subordinates turns around and says "No!"

That is exactly what I had done. I had said no to the injustice and I had said no to taking the hit for others.

Those who had complete power over my career opportunities didn't like it.

Did I regret my decisions? Did I regret saying "No"?

I did not.

Mona Shindy

Chapter 10:
Reflections

Those first days after I parted ways with Navy were lonely. Mohamed and the kids all went off to work and school and I was home by myself. I had a lot of time on my hands to reflect and consider my next steps.

Navy had transferred me to the active Reserves, so it was feasible for me to search for an advertised Reserve position. Essentially, these are roles that business units advertise from time to time, seeking assistance and support to tackle tasks for which they have insufficient or inexperienced staff. They generally run for short durations, equating to a set number of days in the year. I loathed the idea of wearing the Navy uniform ever again. I just did not feel connected to the organisation anymore.

I searched employment ads and found many roles I could do. However, I had lost interest in the idea of working full-time for someone else. It was at that point I decided to dedicate my energy to running my own business. I had run large organisations before and completed many courses, which meant I had the skills to put in place all that was necessary. Starting from scratch, though, is still a huge amount of work.

I loved it.

I worked when I wanted and declined activities that did not align with my interests. I had the freedom to manoeuvre that I had never experienced before.

One of the first activities I chose to tackle was the writing of this book. Besides documenting my experiences and lessons learnt, the authoring was cathartic and gave me the opportunity to collect my thoughts and begin to fully process some of the very difficult experiences of previous years.

We were still dealing with the consequences of a global pandemic and, although its impacts were devastating for many, in other ways it was a welcome distraction from what often felt like an unrelenting international and national focus on people of Islamic faith and their possible ties to terrorism. Muslims, including myself, had weathered suspicion and felt the sting of marginalisation and vilification often fuelled by political rhetoric. For some, we were seen as a threat, while others saw us as a risk probably best steered away from.

In the wake of the Christchurch mosque massacre and attempts to introduce religious freedoms legislation through parliament, I could see national sentiment and mood were gradually changing; not easily or naturally but very much out of necessity. Social cognition theory goes a long way to explaining why particular groups in society are seen and treated a certain way. It explains why some are more easily included and accepted than others.

The Al Noor Mosque massacre in Christchurch on March 15 in 2019 was a real watershed moment for my family and me. I am sure it was for many other Muslim families in the Western world. There was a new sharpness to the dilemma we sometimes struggled with; one where we were feeling unsafe and unwanted in the only societies we knew as home.

I remember watching the horrific news coverage with Mohamed and our girls. We sat in complete silence around the television – shocked, mesmerised and heartbroken. The fifty-one people killed could have just as easily been any one of us, or members of our immediate family. It could have been the mosque next door.

Those in the mosque that day would have been completely oblivious to the imminent threat lurking outside. They would have been completely immersed in their communication with God. In quiet reflection, miles away from the pressures and difficulties of daily life, they would have been seeking forgiveness for any inadequacies and asking the creator for guidance, support, success and comfort in this world and the next. More likely than not, they would have been praying for a better tomorrow, not only for themselves but for all of humanity.

"Why would anyone kill innocent people? People who had done nothing to hurt anyone," my now fifteen-year-old baby asked, fighting back tears.

Mohamed tried to explain. "Some people have deranged ideas, developed and fuelled in echo chambers filled with hate."

"Some hate us so much for no other reason than they have believed the constant media and political rhetoric that tells them all Muslims are a danger and threat to them and their way of life," my oldest added.

"Don't be scared, babes. These types of people are a small minority," I quickly added, trying to reassure my child, who I sensed felt overwhelmingly confused, hurt and helpless. "Most decent humans will be outraged and just as sad as we are. These people will move to help and protect our community. I'm sure of it." I paused. "This world is not always fair or just. Some people have siloed thinking and limited exposure and understanding of others who appear different to them in certain ways. There are many trials that test us in this life. Rest assured, no-one will escape justice in the hereafter."

"But why, Mum? I can get on with so many different friends even though I might not have the same interest in everything they do. What's so hard about it?" my youngest reflected, still not as hardened as the rest of the family had become.

"There is still a fair bit of work humans need to do to dismantle some of the systemic social impediments and barriers that divide communities. It is really important we all continue to mix and include everyone in our circles," I went on. "Right now, unfortunately, some people see Muslims as nothing more than trouble. To be feared and disliked."

Later that evening, I went into my child's room to check on how she was doing. She was still upset and withdrawn, so I curled up in bed with her and held her close until she finally fell asleep.

I had fought for so many years, trying to understand the rationale behind senior officer decisions relating to my management, postings and future career trajectory. Years trying to decipher the often cagey, often non-committal information provided. Years coming to terms with being posted away from my primary areas of expertise, being overlooked for opportunities to prepare for higher rank and having my public exposure significantly curtailed and managed at the highest level within Navy.

I had become something I'd never thought I would be all those years ago when I first signed up – I was 'the problem'. My diversity of perspective was labelled as 'poor judgement' by a homogenous leadership group who all thought alike from a narrow and previously unchallenged viewpoint.

Although the decisions around how I was managed were always framed as 'looking after my interests' and 'protecting me', they resulted in behaviours and outcomes that were inconsistent with how my peers were treated. I had become someone with no agency – recommendations in my favour that could have easily and quickly brought closure to my pain were denied, time and time again.

Providing the support I needed and deserved was too difficult a proposition as it would mean making some real structural and cultural reforms in a conservative organisation ill-equipped to deal with cultural and religious diversity within its ranks.

Maintaining the status quo was easier and quicker; supported by a system that could easily sacrifice an individual.

No questions asked.

Ultimately, after almost eight years of pursuing remedies for emergent health conditions through inefficient Defence Veteran Affairs (DVA) and defective administration claims processes, I am still waiting to achieve a palatable settlement. One that will no doubt be non-disclosable. It has been gruelling and even more damaging than the original trauma. Alongside these very dangerous challenges to a person's mental health that no one should endure, there was also significant change implemented in Defence processes, policy and governance behaviours. Processes were improved to ensure procedural fairness and consultation with affected third parties before the FOI release of personal and private information, Defence social media policy was developed, pastoral care was expanded beyond religious sources and policy was updated relating to support offered to individuals who became the subject of online attacks with an emphasis on better meeting intersecting governance obligations relating to the FOI Act, Privacy Act and WHS Act. Navy also stood up a Diversity and Inclusion Council to progress an inclusion agenda while taking the focus off individual advisers who could be targeted, as I was. These are the things I most value and am incredibly proud to have been the trigger or driver for.

All people face challenges due to biases held by others. Unconscious, affinity and confirmatory biases are real. They can lead to inferior management behaviours and decisions at work, as well as an unwavering rigidity in the friendships and interactions we entertain in our personal lives. These biases are barriers to inter-group integration, understanding and sharing and are phenomenons that should be guarded against.

Such biases result from how we process information through social cognition. These are the processes and structures that affect and are affected by social context. As humans, we have a limited capacity to process information. We use shortcuts to make decisions and are often motivated by our own goals and needs.

The overall impressions we form of people are dominated by stereotypes, unfavourable information, first impressions and personal constructs. We average this information in complex ways, with certain components often influencing understanding and interpretation to dominate the resulting impressions we form. We exclude relevant information and focus instead only on things that confirm our pre-existing beliefs and ideas. This is why very different views may be reached about any given presentation of the same information.

It explains how I can be called a 'terrorist' on my way to work, have it assumed I do not speak English at the checkout while purchasing goods, be pitied by people who believe I am oppressed and need saving from an abusive partner, be ignored by new staff searching for the boss, be hated on for undeservedly being handed opportunities due to apparent tokenism, be accused of being a provocateur for daring to be different, be branded as having devious agendas and then sign multi-million dollar Australian Defence capability and support contracts – all in one day.

It is natural for all of us to be drawn to seeing others as either members of the in-group (i.e. similar to us) or members of a perceived out-group who do not necessarily share all the common standards and customs within our own culture. Those of us having feet in more than one camp can cop it from all sides. As much as I have spoken about my challenges within the Anglo male-dominated military arena,

I also have experienced hostility from elements within the Muslim community, where old patriarchal customs and biases within parts of the community lead some to struggle with the idea of strong women or service in militaries associated with harm brought to their homelands.

In-group and out-group categorisations of people too easily lead to people from minorities being unnoticed, dismissed or overlooked. In some cases, as I have experienced, it can lead to hostility and deliberate attempts to frame and discredit. It means that minority views and voices are not taken seriously. It becomes difficult to exert influence and make a real impact due to being excluded from leadership opportunities or not being acknowledged as able or deserving to lead.

There are some who might ask "Why bother?" Some who "don't care if people of diverse backgrounds get a fair go". It seems like a lot of work for time-strapped leaders to put in place all that is necessary to support what seems like small numbers of diverse participants in the workforce. The answer to this question, of course, is not only that it is everyone's human right to be treated fairly and with respect but it relates to understanding the power and value of diversity and inclusion to business operations and employee growth.

Whether it is trying to determine a marketing approach that appeals to the Australian demographic or a portion of it or just trying to make good general business decisions, a diversity of perspectives brought by a range of people with a different understanding based on life experience and alternate lenses of view leads to better outcomes. Diversity in perspectives helps organisations and communities better identify risks and opportunities. Diversity means increased organisational capability, in terms of improved understanding of customers and collaborators, more creativity and innovation, happier employees, and increased productivity and teamwork to deliver superior outcomes. It is an antidote to 'group think', giving organisations and the nation a competitive edge in an ever-globalised world. We capitalise on the best talent and skills and everyone benefits through personal and professional growth.

It is my experience that whenever an organisation works to integrate diverse employees in new ways and in different settings not previously normalised, the challenges for the individual and entire workforce more broadly are never insignificant. The needed change is often met with friction and resistance. The integration of women on warships in the early '90s and the appointment of myself as a Strategic Adviser on Islamic Cultural affairs in 2013 are two such events I lived through during my Naval career.

Without a doubt, the most important lesson learnt in relation to supporting minorities is the **critical role that leadership plays at all levels** in facilitating and driving change.

Changing prevailing paradigms needs leaders with power and influence to really understand the challenges, the science behind them and to put in place initiatives and support to mitigate the risks, address systemic barriers to inclusion and create the environment and opportunities that give diverse minorities permission to speak and be heard, seen and acknowledged in leadership roles at all stages of their careers. There should be incentives, quotas or targets, that encourage leaders to align with the organisation's diversity and inclusion policies. It is impossible to lead at the highest levels if you have not been supported to lead along the prerequisite stepping stones. By that, I mean supporting minority careers, not just jobs. That requires leaders to mentor and position people from diverse backgrounds in preparation for more senior roles.

Another lesson learnt about how leaders can all work together to drive real change to ensure equity, inclusion and opportunity for all people relates to improving decision-making at all levels of the organisation. Through education, organisations can help employees understand that everyone is on a separate individual journey informed by different inputs; to know we have things to offer others in the world and so much to absorb and learn from them at the same time.

This education is also vital to help support diverse groups feel comfortable sharing their perspectives at work, challenging inappropriate behaviour and not simply mimicking a majority view or approach in order to feel and be accepted. Whenever we mix diverse people, there are great opportunities for collective enrichment but also risks to individuals through the potential loss of identity or hurt through intolerance. Of course, organisations cannot be expected to change all people's biases, but by implementing strategies that minimise their negative impacts, everyone benefits.

We can also improve decision-making by providing the right environment and by reducing time pressures where possible. By structuring and weighting information using evidence, facts and data, we can guard against the brain taking shortcuts. Accountability and consequence procedures through the review and audit of decisions against the company diversity and inclusion policy and having transparency in decision-making where information is processed in an open and constructive manner with elaboration on stimuli or memory can also guard against inherent human biases. Reputation management concerns for organisational leaders and homogeneity in those assessing career management decisions and complaints of unacceptable behaviour can create an inability or reluctance to highlight disadvantages and inequitable outcomes for minority groups. That is why the Diversity Council of Australia, in their 2022 report, *Racism in the Workplace*, made recommendations that decisions regarding complaints made by Culturally and Linguistically Diverse (CALD) people should be independently assessed by experts with cultural and race competencies. This is to address problems that often arise where reviewing entities, even apparently independent HR practitioners, still have strong allegiances to the organisation.

Finally, effective communication and how information is delivered in difficult environments are crucial to success in this space. Timeframes are important when it comes to communication and the acceptance of that communication in difficult environments. Tone, language, the medium used and adequate opportunity for deeper and more sophisticated discussion with clarifications and evidence is needed for the introduction of new perspectives. Besides communication, the pace of actual change is also important. Conservative organisations sometimes struggle to accept and absorb change if it comes too quickly. Patience and resilience are key attributes for change agents.

My experiences have taught me that we are certainly all much more similar than we are different. The more we open ourselves up to looking, learning and sharing, the more we are able to not only begin to understand and appreciate individual differences but to celebrate them as something that benefits us all.

That said, being at the vanguard of any reform or change is always difficult. The adventure can be quite testing, but the potential rewards are amazing and long-lasting. Expect to get dirty.

Final Words

I am sure that when some people picked up this book, read its title and married it up with the cover picture of a Muslim woman in an Australian Navy uniform, pre-conceived beliefs would have intrigued them and led them to wonder about its authenticity. Those attitudes and biases, and the structural frameworks, beliefs and norms that reinforce them, are the very things that this book has explored. They are the things that are detrimental to personal and organisational excellence and that must be challenged and dismantled if we are to grow and excel as a nation effectively, supported by all citizens and important national institutions.

The book has captured my military career journey. It was written to document my experiences and lessons learnt along the way in the hope I might inspire people just like me – minorities – to overcome their own doubts as they pursue their life and career goals. This is important because these doubts can be amongst our strongest enemies as they erode personal resilience, persistence and endurance.

My story teaches what it takes to challenge and dismantle pre-conceived beliefs and longstanding structural norms within traditionally conservative institutions.

It teaches that leaders must not ask minorities to step up and pay the price. Input from minorities is critical for success, but leaders must be prepared to provide support, backup and protection when needed. Too often, minorities are discarded as sacrificial lambs in the exercising of policy that is driven more by trendy agendas or to argue progress, than well-consulted and researched facts and risk analysis.

Mona Shindy

I am reminded of the words delivered by a very senior military officer who was briefing my cohort of strategic leaders at the Australian Defence College in 2016: "It is really hard to get your arms around someone who has well and truly been smothered in shit!"

Although I can understand his explanation, describing why leaders may be reluctant to openly support someone who has been targeted and smeared, it is simply not good enough. True leadership involves taking decisive action from the front and the service of subordinates to ensure safe and productive work environments.

When internal policy and work practices support the incontestable behaviour of powerful networks, they act as formidable barriers to an institution's ability to perform at its very best. When an organisation grows disgruntled and damaged employees, who may underperform or prematurely resign due to poor utilisation of the most appropriate talent pool in decision-making positions of influence that require diversity of thought and perspective, it inadvertently limits its potential success and growth. With no incentive or understanding of the need to change, a lack of transparency and accountability become the cornerstones of behaviour most fiercely defended by those entrusted to govern and lead. Unchecked and unchallenged, such constructs can allow misconduct and unfairness to fester. You only need to look at the Brereton Inquiry into alleged war crimes in Afghanistan and the current Royal Commission into Defence and Veteran Suicide to see this at work.

The change journey can be extremely difficult and painful. It requires leaders to be open-minded, individuals to have the courage to speak truth to power and the appropriate structural supports that will facilitate acknowledgement and action against those truths. Equitable policy and processes that allow no group or person to be untouchable or unchallengeable, and that support independently contestable promotion, reward, punishment or non-punishment, are essential for the health and required performance of our nation's greatest institutions.

My experiences in the military have been amazing. They have supported my personal development and professional growth. I have met and made incredible lifelong friends through the experience and will always be grateful for what it has given me. With the triumphs and rewards, there have been just as many disappointments and difficulties that have challenged my trust, loyalty, health and connection with the institution along the way. I wrote this book just after separating from my permanent Navy role to collate my thoughts while reflecting on what, in the main, was a highly rewarding career. The book was also the starting point and foundation for my work moving forward. It is important to me to give back from what I have gained and learned.

Now as the CEO of my own organisation, Mona Shindy Consulting, I impart knowledge and teach resilience and growth techniques to individuals through mentoring. More specifically, I seek to inspire and support minorities through speaking engagements that gather and serve communities or at academic and youth development institutions. An arm of my business also acts as a social enterprise, providing grants to support the advancement of girls and boys from minority groups.

Concurrently, I speak and consult with organisations that are serious about understanding blind spots and implementing necessary structural changes to supercharge growth and success through a happy, appropriately diverse and effectively-utilised workforce. Through dedicated consulting and an array of short courses, I provide tools that assist organisations in identifying and correcting systemic structural deficiencies.

To get in contact or learn more about my activities, my other books or those I am currently writing, go to *www.monashindy.com*

Mona Shindy

References

The Australian. 2016. "Navy Officer 'Crossed The Line'", 2016. https://www.theaustralian.com.au/.

"A Clarification". 2016. Austeralix Journals. https://austeralix.com/2016/04/26/a-clarification/.

"Walk The Plank | The Spectator Australia". 2016. The Spectator Australia. https://www.spectator.com.au/2016/04/walk-the-plank/.

Mona Shindy

Mona Shindy

www.ingramcontent.com/pod-product-compliance
Lightning Source LLC
Chambersburg PA
CBHW071833230426
43671CB00012B/1945